Frequently Asked Questions

Japan FAQ

by David Thayne

Level 4
(2000-word)

IBC パブリッシング

はじめに

　ラダーシリーズは、「はしご（ladder）」を使って一歩一歩上を目指すように、学習者の実力に合わせ、無理なくステップアップできるよう開発された英文リーダーのシリーズです。

　リーディング力をつけるためには、繰り返したくさん読むこと、いわゆる「多読」がもっとも効果的な学習法であると言われています。多読では、「1.速く 2.訳さず英語のまま 3.なるべく辞書を使わず」に読むことが大切です。スピードを計るなど、速く読むよう心がけましょう（たとえばTOEIC®テストの音声スピードはおよそ1分間に150語です）。そして1語ずつ訳すのではなく、英語を英語のまま理解するくせをつけるようにします。こうして読み続けるうちに語感がついてきて、だんだんと英語が理解できるようになるのです。まずは、ラダーシリーズの中からあなたのレベルに合った本を選び、少しずつ英文に慣れ親しんでください。たくさんの本を手にとるうちに、英文書がすらすら読めるようになってくるはずです。

《本シリーズの特徴》
- 中学校レベルから中級者レベルまで5段階に分かれています。自分にあったレベルからスタートしてください。
- クラシックから現代文学、ノンフィクション、ビジネスと幅広いジャンルを扱っています。あなたの興味に合わせてタイトルを選べます。
- 巻末のワードリストで、いつでもどこでも単語の意味を確認できます。レベル1、2では、文中の全ての単語が、レベル3以上は中学校レベル外の単語が掲載されています。
- カバーにヘッドホーンマークのついているタイトルは、オーディオ・サポートがあります。ウェブから購入／ダウンロードし、リスニング教材としても併用できます。

《使用語彙について》
レベル1：中学校で学習する単語約1000語
レベル2：レベル1の単語＋使用頻度の高い単語約300語
レベル3：レベル1の単語＋使用頻度の高い単語約600語
レベル4：レベル1の単語＋使用頻度の高い単語約1000語
レベル5：語彙制限なし

Introduction

I remember when I first got off the airplane at Narita airport more than 20 years ago. I felt like I was on a different planet! Everything I saw was new and exotic. My head was filled with questions and I wanted to know everything. I wanted to know about the country, the language, the land, the government, and how Japanese think.

Whenever I met people who spoke a little English, I would ask them questions about Japan. Some people were very helpful and could give me a lot of answers. Other people didn't seem to know even basic information about their own country!

Why I wrote this book

When you talk to someone from another country, you never know what topic will come up. If you know what you're going to talk about, then you can prepare by learning new words and phrases. If you are Japanese, one topic that will almost always come up is Japan itself, and you should be able to talk about your own country.

How I picked these questions

Many of the questions in this book are questions that I asked myself. Other questions are questions that people asked me when they learned I lived in Japan. If you talk to non-Japanese people, they will probably ask you one or more of these questions. And these are all questions that Japanese should be able to answer.

What people want to know about Japan

When people become interested in Japan, they want to know not only facts and figures, but also how the Japanese think and why they think that way. In this book, I have also included some of my own experiences. I hope that this will help you to share your own experiences. Although it's important to know the basics, people can find all those things in an encyclopedia or on the Internet. It's more important that you express your feelings and talk about your experiences.

You might have an opportunity to show someone around Japan. You might go abroad on a trip or to live for some time. By talking more about Japan, you will be able to improve your English. You will also learn more about other countries and other people and their experiences.

Best of luck!
David Thayne

CONTENTS

Part 1 **The Basic Facts and Figures** 1

1. The Basic Facts and Figures *3*
2. Japanese History *18*
3. The Japanese Language *28*
4. The Imperial Family *33*

Part 2 **Japanese Society** 39

1. Japanese Government *41*
2. Japanese Economy *54*
3. Social Issues in Japan *58*
4. Japanese at Work *66*
5. Japanese in School....*76*

Part 3 **Japanese Life and Culture** 85

1. Japanese at Home *87*
2. Japanese Ceremonies *98*
3. Japanese Food *102*
4. Traveling in Japan *112*
5. Japanese Leisure....*123*
6. Japanese Tradition *129*
7. Japanese Custom *143*

Word List...156

Part 1

The Basic Facts and Figures

読みはじめる前に

Part 1 で使われている用語です。わからない語は巻末のワードリストで確認しましょう。

- [ ] anthem
- [ ] capital
- [ ] climate
- [ ] constitution
- [ ] disaster
- [ ] earthquake
- [ ] emperor
- [ ] figure
- [ ] geography
- [ ] imperial
- [ ] latitude
- [ ] military
- [ ] monarchy
- [ ] population
- [ ] region
- [ ] temperature
- [ ] typhoon
- [ ] volcano

知っておきたい基本情報

日本の人口
日本の人口は約1億2750万人で、世界第9位。世界で最も人口が多いのは中国で、約12億9440万人 (2002年)。

日本の面積
日本の面積は約37万7880km²で、イタリアやドイツより広い。

日本の位置
日本は約3798kmと、南北に長いのが特徴。緯度は青島 (中国)、テヘラン (イラン)、グランドキャニオン (アメリカ) などと同じくらい、経度はニューギニアなどと同じ。

日本の自然災害
地震、台風、火山の噴火が多い日本。台風は年間27くらい発生し、全国に富士山を含む80以上の活火山がある。

日本の言葉
漢字は1400年ほど前に中国から伝わったとされ、日本独自の漢字も作られた。現在、文部科学省は1945字の常用漢字を定めている。

1 The Basic Facts and Figures

Q What kind of country is Japan?

The most notable feature of Japan is that it is an island country. Being an island is not only about the geography. Some people think living in an island country changes the way people think. For example, it is said that Japanese people have *shimaguni-konjo*. They think they are something special and sometimes don't let other people join their society.

Because Japan is an island country, it has a unique culture. Some parts of Japanese culture, such as kimono and *ninja*, are known throughout the world.

Many people know about Japanese history from watching movies about samurai. In 1980, there was a famous book and a movie called *Shogun*. Then, in 2003, *The Last Samurai* became another popular movie about Japan. These movies were not accurate in every way, but they did help to create a lot of interest in Japan.

Another thing that Japan is famous for is *manga* (comics) and *anime* (animated cartoons). In most countries, people lose interest in cartoons when they get older, so most of the stories are for children. But in Japan, many people, even adults, are fans of *manga* and *anime*. For this reason, Japanese *manga* and *anime* stories are more mature. This has made *manga* and *anime* well known in many countries of the world.

There are also some foods that have made Japan famous. For example, many people have tried such foods as tofu, sushi, sukiyaki and tempura. Japanese food is popular, not only because it's unique, but also because it's healthy.

❏ Population

Q What is the population of Japan?

Japan's population was 127.5 million in 2002. This means that Japan has the ninth-largest population in the world. The country with the biggest population in the world is China with 1.294 billion, followed by India with 1.041 billion. The United States has the third largest population with 285.5 million.

The population is high compared with the land area. In Japan, there are 342 people per square kilometer. This is almost the same as small countries in Europe. In Australia, there are only 2.29 people per square kilometer!

Half of the people in Japan live in three big cities: Tokyo, Nagoya, and Osaka. This makes Japan seem like a small country. Japanese live in the cities because most of the country is covered in mountains.

If you get on a train in Tokyo and go to Nagoya or Osaka, most of the way you can see houses and buildings. It makes you think that there is nothing but buildings in Japan. But if you travel in a car or on a local train line, you will soon see that there are lots of mountains and nature in Japan. In fact, there are many places to go camping, fishing, or hiking only an hour or so away from central Tokyo.

Q Is the Japanese population changing?

Japan is one of the few countries in the world where the population is decreasing. This is because only 1.1

million babies are born each year and the number is expected to drop even more.

Concerning the population of males and females at birth, there are 1.05 males for every female. But at age 65, there are only 0.72 males for each female. In the total population, there are 0.96 males for each female.

Currently, the biggest concern about the Japanese population is aging. Although the population is going down, the number of elderly people is growing. It is now estimated that about 20% of the population is 65 or older.

❏ Geography

Q Is Japan really a small country?

When I first came to Japan, I remember someone saying to me, "Japan is a narrow country." That seemed to make sense because the shape of Japan is long and narrow. But now I know that what he wanted to say was "Japan is a small country." The word *semai* in Japanese can mean "small," but it is often translated as "narrow." To native English speakers, a narrow

Total Area

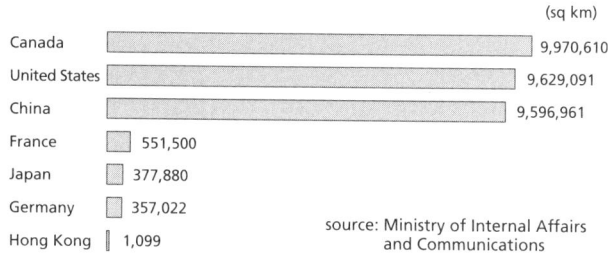

country can be quite big, but just not very wide across.

Japan is not a small country if you compare the figures. The total area of Japan is 377,880 square kilometers (146,000 square miles), which makes it larger than Italy or Germany. The main island, Honshu, is slightly larger than the United Kingdom.

Of course, there are some countries which are much bigger than Japan. Japan is only one twenty-fifth the size of China and the United States.

Q Where is Japan?

The nation of Japan is a long, narrow chain of islands on the western side of the North Pacific Ocean on the eastern edge of the Asian continent.

It is about 3,798 kilometers (2,360 miles) long northeast to southwest. If Japan were placed on top of the eastern coast of North America, it would run from Montreal, Canada in the north, to Jacksonville, Florida, in the south.

Tokyo, the capital of Japan, is on the same latitude as Tsingtao, Teheran, Malta, the Strait of Gibraltar, and the Grand Canyon, and the same longitude as New Guinea and central Australia.

Japan is surrounded by the Pacific Ocean and the Japan Sea. The nearest countries to the west and north are China, Korea, and Russia.

Q Could you tell me about the geography of Japan?

There are four major islands. They are Honshu (89,194 square miles), Hokkaido (32,246), Kyushu (17,135) and Shikoku (7,258). These four main islands make up about 98% of Japan's total land area. There are also thousands of small islands. In fact, Japan has 7,000 islands, but no people live on most of them.

PART 1 THE BASIC FACTS AND FIGURES

Q Are there regional differences in Japan?

Yes. Everywhere you go in Japan, you can find differences.

Japan is usually divided into 11 regions: Hokkaido, Tohoku, Kanto, Shinetsu, Tokai, Hokuriku, Kinki, Chugoku, Shikoku, Kyushu, and Okinawa. The culture, and even the language, is slightly different in each region.

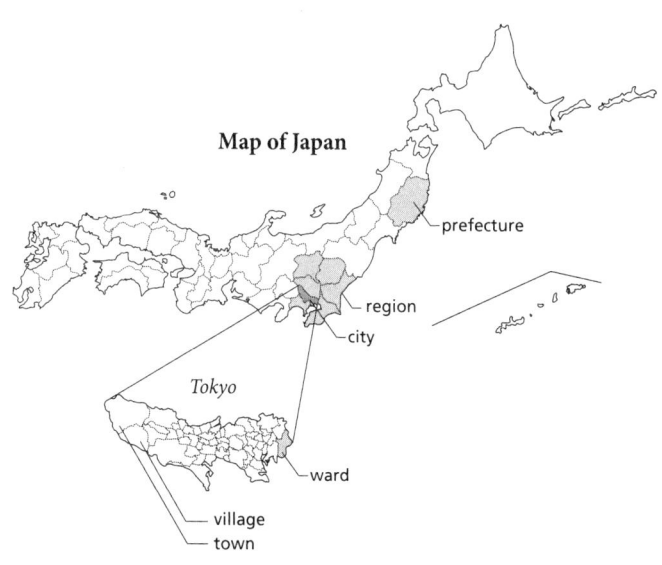

Map of Japan

If you travel around Japan, you can enjoy the differences in local art and cuisine. For example, in the Kanto area the flavor of the food is salty, with a soy-sauce flavor. In Kansai, the flavor of the food is more delicate and sweeter.

Many people say that you can judge what part of the country a person comes from by his or her personality. For example, people from Kyushu and Okinawa are very passionate, and people from Tohoku and Hokkaido are rather patient.

❑ Climate

Q What is the climate of Japan like?

Japan has four seasons, similar to America and Europe. The winter months (December to February) are the coldest, and the summer months (July to September) are the hottest. In Tokyo, the coldest winter temperature on record is minus 9°C (15.8°F) and the hottest temperature on record is 39.5°C (103.1°F)

As Japan is a long, narrow country, the temperature varies a lot from north to south, even on the same day.

Part 1 The Basic Facts and Figures

Sometimes my friends from America ask what the weather is like in Japan, but it's a difficult question to answer. The northern part can be as cold as Alaska, and the southern part can be as warm as Hawaii.

Q Can you tell me more about the seasons in Japan?

For most of Japan, there are four distinct seasons.

Spring

Spring is one of the best times to visit Japan, because you can see beautiful blossoms. Japanese cherry blossoms are famous throughout the world. They usually start to bloom in southern Japan at the end of March. The "cherry blossom front" gradually moves north, so although the blossoms only last for one week in each area, the season lasts for nearly three months in total.

I remember my first cherry blossom season in Japan. I thought Japanese were always very shy in public. But I saw a different side of the Japanese under the cherry trees. People were sitting on the ground and talking, drinking, and dancing around.

In fact, during the cherry blossom time, there are people everywhere. Some of them even go to the park and stake out their spots under the cherry trees days before the blossoms come out. It's like a big party and everyone is having a good time. If you walk around, a group of people will probably ask you to join them.

Summer

After the rainy season, it becomes very hot and humid. Recently, the summers are warmer and many people worry about global warming,  especially in the big cities. But one way to forget the heat is to go to a festival. There are many festivals in summer. The O-bon dance festivals and firework displays are especially popular.

Autumn

Many people who come to Japan think autumn is the best season. The weather is mild and the leaves on the trees turn a beautiful red. There are also a lot of autumn festivals from early September to early November, including the "moon viewing" festival.

Winter

Winter is very different in each area. Toward the end of November, cold winds bring rain and snow from Siberia. These affect the side of the country on the coast of the Japan Sea. The most snow falls in the Hokuriku region (Fukui, Ishikawa, Toyama and Niigata prefectures).

Areas on the Pacific Ocean coast have much milder weather. For example, the average temperature in Tokyo in winter is only about 5°C. Luckily, there are hot springs almost everywhere you go in Japan. And one of the best things in the world is a hot-spring bath in the middle of the winter!

Q Does it rain a lot in Japan?

Most rain falls during the "rainy season", from early June to the middle of July. This time of the year is called *tsuyu*.

The average rainfall during June is 185 millimeters. It doesn't usually rain hard every day. It rains on and off. The famous professor Donald Keene once said that Japan has five seasons—the extra one being *tsuyu*. During this time, it's sometimes very hot and rainy, so it's not very comfortable at all. But sometimes the clouds clear up and the weather is quite nice.

❑ Natural Disasters

Q Are there a lot of earthquakes in Japan?

Yes. Japan is located on several plates that cause earthquakes when they move. The plates surrounding the Pacific Ocean are known as the Ring of Fire.

Because of this, there are a lot of earthquakes and volcanoes compared with other countries. Most people who move to Japan remember their first earthquake. I was teaching English, and when the earthquake hit, I wanted to run outside. But all the students just kept on talking like nothing was happening. I'm glad it was only a little earthquake.

Part 1 The Basic Facts and Figures

Q Is it true that Japan has its own eathquake scale?

Yes, it is. In most countries, the Richter scale is used to define the size of an earthquake. It measures the amount of energy an earthquake releases at its epicenter.

But in Japan, the *shindo* scale is more commonly used. *Shindo* refers to the intensity of an earthquake at one location. This makes it easier to understand how much shaking is felt by people in different places.

A slight earthquake only felt by a few people who are standing still is 1 on the scale. 2 and 3 are still minor earthquakes that do not cause damage. But at 4, objects start to fall, and even greater damage occurs at 5 and 6. 7 is a serious earthquake.

Q What was the biggest earthquake to ever hit Japan?

The worst earthquake in modern Japanese history was the Great Kanto Earthquake in 1923. It was magnitude 7.9 and 142,800 people were killed or went missing.

On January 17, 1995, at 5:46 a.m., the Great

Hanshin Earthquake in Kobe killed over 6,000 people. It measured about 7 on the Japanese scale. It was the worst disaster in Japan since the end of World War II. Japan learned a lot from this earthquake. The country is trying to become better-prepared for earthquakes and other disasters.

The most serious earthquake recently was on October 23, 2004. The Niigata Chuetsu Earthquake registered 7 on the Japanese scale (6.8 on the Richter scale). It killed 40 people, injured over 4,000 people, and caused a lot of damage. It was the first time in history that a Shinkansen bullet train was derailed, but no one on the train was injured.

Q Are there a lot of typhoons in Japan?

Yes. Although typhoons can hit Japan in any month of the year, the main typhoon season is from May to November. Most typhoons come in August and September. In an average year, there are approximately 27 typhoons, but only about three hit the main part of Japan. Typhoons are especially common in the southern part of Japan. They sometimes cause serious damage.

PART 1 THE BASIC FACTS AND FIGURES

Q What is the difference between a typhoon and a hurricane?

"Typhoon" and "hurricane" are two names for the same thing. They are both tropical cyclones with winds of 120 kilometers per hour or stronger. When these storms take place in the Atlantic Ocean, the Caribbean Sea, and the Gulf of Mexico, they are called hurricanes. When they occur in the North Pacific Ocean west of the International Date Line, they are called typhoons.

Q Are there a lot of volcanoes in Japan?

Yes. In fact, 10% of the world's active volcanoes are in Japan. There are over 80 active volcanoes, including Mount Fuji, and hundreds of sleeping volcanoes. The Japanese government studies the live volcanoes closely. It hopes to be able to predict when they will erupt, so that people living nearby can be warned.

2 Japanese History

❏ Ancient History

Q How far back can Japanese history be traced?

The Jomon Prehistoric Period lasted from 10,000 B.C. to 300 B.C. Most of the things left from this period are pottery and tools. Researchers recently discovered there may have been a well-organized society, but we don't know very much about the period.

During this time, Japan was not really a country. It was made up of tribes and clans. There are myths that speak of Jimmu, a descendant of Amaterasu Omikami, the sun goddess. He is said to have founded Japan in 660 B.C. and became the first emperor of Japan.

Q How did Japan become a country?

During the Kofun Period, some clan rulers gained

a lot of power. This is when the Imperial dynasty started. Prince Shotoku was born to Emperor Yomei in 574 A.D. He liked to learn about China because it was one of the most developed countries in the world. And he wanted to make a government in Japan that was like the government in China at that time. It was during this period that the Japanese brought the *kanji* writing system from China. In 604 A.D., Prince Shotoku created a constitution with 17 articles. This is the oldest written law in Japan.

❑ Middle Ages

Q How did the warlords gain power in Japan?

For many years, the emperor had the most power in Japan, but after Minamoto no Yoritomo established his Kamakura government in 1192, the military gradually started to gain power. The emperor remained as a symbol of power, but the real power was held by the warlords.

Q What was the Sengoku Period?

The Sengoku Period or "Warring-States" period, was a time of civil war that lasted from the middle of the 15th century to the early 17th century.

Oda Nobunaga was a powerful warlord. He fought many wars to unify the country, but he was assassinated in 1582. Then another powerful lord called Toyotomi Hideyoshi gained power. In 1590, he united all of Japan. Hideyoshi died in 1598, and then his retainer, Tokugawa Ieyasu, became the leader. In the Battle of Sekigahara in 1600, Ieyasu defeated his main enemies and became the ruler of the country. He established the Edo government and during the Edo Period (1603–1867), peace finally returned to Japan.

Q What happened during the Edo Period?

Tokugawa Ieyasu set up a social system with samurai at the top, followed by farmers, artisans and merchants. In order to keep stability, he forced all foreigners to leave Japan and made it against the law to deal with foreigners. This is called the "national isolation period." It lasted until 1853, when an American, Matthew C. Perry, came to Japan with his ships.

❑ Modern History

Q When did Japan's modern history begin?

Some foreigners in Japan know a lot about the country and its culture, but others don't know very much at all. I once met a man who had just come to Japan. He said that he was so disappointed because he couldn't find any samurai or *ninja*.

The samurai disappeared in Japan when the emperor took power again and the Meiji Period started. It lasted from 1868 to 1912. During this period, Japan worked hard to become a modern country and a world power.

In a very short period of time, the country made great progress. One reason that Japan could change so quickly was the employment of 3,000 foreign experts by the government. These people came to Japan and taught such topics as English, engineering, and science. During this period, many students also left Japan and went to study in America and Europe. The government helped to support the progress by giving money to people and companies. Large *zaibatsu* such as Mitsubishi and Mitsui gained a lot of power during this time. In order for the country to continue to grow, Japan began to export and import from other Asian countries.

In the Sino-Japanese War (1894–1895), Japan defeated China in Korea. In 1902, Japan signed the Anglo-Japanese Alliance and then won the Russo-Japanese War (1904–1905) against Russia in Manchuria. In the first World War, it took over the German-held territory in China and the Pacific.

Q Why did Japan get into World War II?

After the first World War, Europe was weak and lost much of its influence in Asia. Japan was quite strong at this time and it opened up new opportunities.

But America was afraid that Japan would become too strong. America started to get in the way of Japan in Asia. The military in Japan was very strong at that time and it decided to attack Pearl Harbor in Hawaii. Some people in the government tried to stop them, but the military was too strong.

Q How did Japan change after the war?

During the war, many people were willing to die for the country and for the emperor. It was believed by almost everyone that the emperor was a god. But after the war, people realized that they had been tricked into supporting the war. People continue to respect the emperor as a symbol of Japan, but they no longer think of the emperor as a god.

At the end of the war, the economy was almost completely destroyed. Most people were very poor and it was difficult just to survive. But the Japanese worked very hard to rebuild the country. They experienced rapid economic growth from the mid-1950s to the end of the 1960s.

The Summer Olympics were held in Tokyo in 1964, and Japan became a member of the OECD in the same year. By the 1980s, Japan was once again one of the strongest powers in the world. Many people think that one of the reasons Japan was able to become strong was the close cooperation between the government and companies.

Q What type of government does Japan have?

The government that Japan has now is a constitutional monarchy. After World War II, Emperor Hirohito (now known as Emperor Showa) told the people that he was not a god and would stay on only as a symbol in Japan.

Q How did the Constitution of Japan come into being?

After World War II, the United States Forces were all over the country. From 1945 to 1952, General Douglas MacArthur was the Supreme Commander of Allied Forces. Under him, a new constitution was made in 1947.

The new Constitution stated that Japan would never go to war again. The San Francisco Peace Treaty ended the Occupation in 1952, and Okinawa was given back to Japan in 1972.

There is now a lot of discussion about the Constitution. Many people think it should be changed in order to keep up with the changes going on in the world. But there are also a lot of people who think that changing the Constitution will make it easier for Japan to go to war again.

Q Does Japan get along well with other countries in Asia?

Unfortunately, there are a lot of problems that need to be dealt with.

Many countries in Asia do not have positive feelings towards Japan because they think Japan has not properly apologized for war crimes during World War II and before. Japan donates a lot of money and aid to Asian countries, but it has been difficult for the country to give a clear apology.

But younger Japanese do not seem to care so much about the past. Ties between Japan and South Korea, especially, have gotten much better in recent years.

Q What is the national anthem of Japan?

It's called *Kimigayo* or "The Emperor's Reign." It was made the national anthem in 1888. The music was written in 1880 by Hiromori Hayashi, an imperial court musician.

The words of the anthem are a *tanka* (5-line, 31-syllable poem) based on a 10th-century collection.

The words are as follows:
> *Kimi ga yo wa*
> *Chiyo ni yachiyo ni*
> *Sazare ishi no*
> *Iwao to nari te*
> *Koke no musu made.*

Here is an English translation:
> May the reign of the Emperor
> continue for a thousand, nay, eight thousand generations
> and for the eternity that it takes
> for small pebbles to grow into a great rock
> and become covered with moss.

Part 1 The Basic Facts and Figures

Q Could you tell me about the Japanese flag?

The Japanese flag is simply a large red circle on a white background. It is called the *Hinomaru*, which means "sun disk." It has been used as a national symbol since at least the 17th century. The *Hinomaru* was made Japan's official national flag in August 1999.

When I first came to Japan, I remember someone talking about *hinomaru bento*. This sounded strange to me, and I couldn't find the meaning in a dictionary. I finally learned that it is a container of rice with a red pickled plum in the center.

3 The Japanese Language

Q Where did *kanji* come from?

Kanji, or Chinese characters, came from China about 1,400 years ago. Similar *kanji* are also used in China, Korea, Taiwan and other countries, but they don't have the same meaning. For example, the characters for "letter" *(tegami)* mean "toilet paper" in China.

There are two types of *kanji* in Japanese. One type is close to the Chinese characters that came from China. The other type is called "Japanese *kanji*" *(kokuji)*. *Kokuji* were made by Japanese based on Chinese characters. Japanese characters are simpler than Chinese characters.

In 1981, the former Ministry of Education, Science, Sports and Culture, designated 1,945 *kanji* for daily use. They are called *joyo-kanji*. They are learned in school, so most people know at least this many characters.

Q Is Japanese a difficult language to learn?

There are only 51 sounds in Japanese, so it is not difficult to pronounce. Some people say that Japanese sounds like Spanish.

However, there are many types of Japanese, and so it is difficult to know which type to use. Male and female Japanese is a bit different, so if a man uses the language used by women, he will sound very strange. Or if an adult used the language used by a child, that would sound funny.

It is easy to speak basic Japanese, but it is very difficult to speak correct, polite Japanese. For example, there are sometimes many ways to say one thing. If you want to say "you", you can use *anata*, *kimi* or *omae*. You have to use the right word or you will sound too strong or too weak.

For me, one of the most difficult things about

learning Japanese was knowing which word to use. It took me a long time to learn that it was okay to say *omae* to a friend, but not to a business client. I had an American friend who told me he once called his Japanese client *omae* because he was in the habit of using it all the time with his friends! Of course, this didn't sound good at all.

In America and many other countries, the most important thing is to be friendly. So it's not uncommon to even call your boss by his or her first name. But in Japan, it's more important to show respect than to be friendly. So sometimes you might think that Japanese are unfriendly and cold, but they are probably just trying to show respect to you.

Q Is Japanese difficult to read and write?

Yes, it is difficult. One of the reasons is that there are three types of writing: *kanji, hiragana* and *katakana*.

Each *kanji* character has a meaning, and the characters are put together to form words. For example, the *kanji* for "food" is made by putting the character for "to eat" and the character for "thing" together to make "an eating thing."

To write the *kanji* for "America," you first write the character for "rice" and then the character for "country." If you know about 2,000 *kanji*, you can probably read a newspaper.

Hiragana is like simple *kanji*. The *hiragana* symbols are a little like the English alphabet because they have sounds and not meanings. These symbols are used to put *kanji* together and to show different forms of the same root *kanji*. For example: in *haya-i* ("quick," adjective), *haya-ku* ("quickly," adverb), *haya-sa* ("speed," noun), the *haya* part is the *kanji* and the rest is written in *hiragana*. And *hiragana* can also be used to make words on their own.

Katakana is like *hiragana*: each symbol has a sound and not a meaning. But *katakana* is used mostly to write words from English or other Western languages. So if you wanted to write "hamburger" in Japanese, you would use *katakana*.

Q: Can you pronounce Western names properly in Japanese?

Japanese has fewer sounds than English, and so when you put names into Japanese, you can sometimes get funny words. For example, my family name is Thayne, but I have to pronounce it "Sein" in Japanese. Sometimes when I call people on the telephone for the first time, they think I said "My name is Hussein," as in Saddam Hussein.

Other foreigners have an even more difficult time with their names in Japan. I met a man in Japan named Gerry. In Japanese his name sounds like *geri* (diarrhea). Another one is "Barker," which sounds like *baka* (fool).

4 The Imperial Family

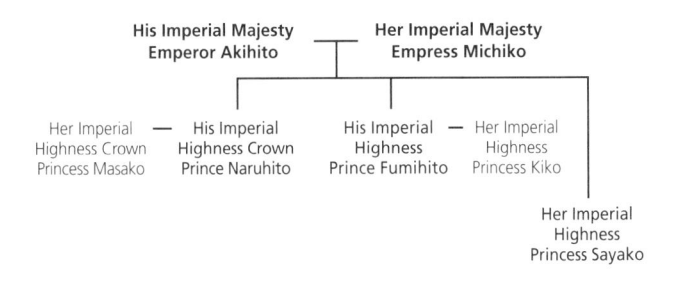

```
            His Imperial Majesty ——— Her Imperial Majesty
            Emperor Akihito              Empress Michiko
    ┌──────────────────┬──────────────────────┐
Her Imperial  —  His Imperial     His Imperial  —  Her Imperial
Highness Crown   Highness Crown    Highness         Highness
Princess Masako  Prince Naruhito   Prince Fumihito  Princess Kiko

                                          Her Imperial
                                          Highness
                                          Princess Sayako
```

Q Does the emperor have any power over the government?

Chapter I of the 1947 Constitution of Japan establishes what the emperor can and can't do. It says that the emperor is the symbol of the country. Article 7 says that the emperor can act as the head of state with the advice and approval of the Cabinet. The emperor performs many of the roles of a head of state. The emperor works as a diplomat for Japan and is seen as the head of state by foreign governments. Also, all the prime ministers have to be designated by the emperor, although they are chosen by the political party with the most power.

Q What do the Emperor and Empress do?

The imperial family attends many events all year around. They host many ceremonies, lunches, and dinners and they meet a large number of people from other countries, such as scientists and artists. So far, they have made official visits to over 14 countries.

In all the years I have lived in Japan, I've only seen Empress Michiko once. I was walking down the street and people started to line up waiting for something. I asked someone what was happening, and I was told that the Empress would be coming by in a car soon. I waited a few minutes and she drove right by. She had the window down and was waving at people. She appeared very humble and also very elegant. I could see that she does represent many of the traits that Japanese value.

Q What is the enthronement ceremony?

It is called the *Daijosai*, and is held to bring into existence a new emperor in accordance with the spirit of the ancient Japanese goddess, Amaterasu Omikami. It is the most important ceremony for the imperial family.

The origin of this ceremony is written about in the myths of *Tensonkorin* (The Descent to Earth of the Descendants of the Sun Goddess) and *Jimmu Tenno Tosei*, (The Eastern Expedition of Emperor Jimmu) in the *Kojiki*, a Japanese ancient history book.

Q Can princes marry commoners?

Yes. On April 10, 1959, Crown Prince Akihito married Michiko Shoda, the daughter of a businessman. It was one of the happiest days in the history of Japan. Dr. Shinzo Koizumi, who taught the Crown Prince for many years, said of this marriage, "The Crown Prince chose her, and so did we."

In the past, it was almost unheard of for a prince to marry a commoner, but times have changed. The

Emperor and Empress are very popular with the Japanese people. The future emperor, Crown Prince Hironomiya, also chose to marry a commoner. Crown Princess Masako is a former diplomat.

Q Where does the imperial family live?

The Emperor and Empress live at the Imperial Palace in the middle of Tokyo. The current Imperial Palace is on the site of the old Edo Castle. There is a large park area around it. You can see moats and massive stone walls. It is a short walk from Tokyo Station.

Edo Castle was the seat of the Tokugawa shoguns, who ruled over Japan from 1603 until 1867. In 1868, the shogunate was overthrown, and construction of a new Imperial Palace was completed in 1888.

Q Can you go inside the Imperial Palace?

The palace buildings and inner gardens are not open to the public, except on January 2 (New Year's Greeting) and December 23 (Emperor's Birthday), when visitors can go into the grounds of the inner palace and see the members of the imperial family greet the people.

During the rest of the year, you can make reservations with the Imperial Household Agency for a tour. Tours of the palace are given in Japanese, with an English pamphlet.

When you walk around the Imperial Palace, you will notice that there are no recognizable monuments.

It seems that most countries have really famous spots that are big like the Statue of Liberty in America, the Eiffel Tower in France, and Big Ben in England. But in Japan, there are very few really big, famous, historical places, except for maybe Mt. Fuji. Even the Giant Buddha statue in Kamakura is only a few meters tall. After living in Japan for several years, I learned that the Japanese are able to see beauty and have pride in small and simple things. Once you learn this, you will be able to enjoy Japan a lot more.

Part 2

Japanese Society

読みはじめる前に

Part 2 で使われている用語です。わからない語は巻末のワードリストで確認しましょう。

- [ ] arrest
- [ ] birthrate
- [ ] Cabinet
- [ ] court
- [ ] crime
- [ ] Diet
- [ ] economy
- [ ] education
- [ ] election
- [ ] exam
- [ ] export
- [ ] government
- [ ] import
- [ ] income
- [ ] labor
- [ ] legislative
- [ ] minister
- [ ] politics
- [ ] trading
- [ ] unemployment
- [ ] vote

知っておきたい基本情報

日本の国会

日本の国会は衆議院(House of Representatives)と参議院(House of Councilors)からなり、衆議院の定数480のうち300は小選挙区から選出され、180は比例代表選出。参議院は定数242で、146は選挙区から、残り96は比例代表で選出される。

日本の犯罪

2003年の日本の犯罪件数は、約279万件と、10年前に比べ、100万件近く増えている。反対に、検挙数は72万件から64万件へと減少している。

日本の労働者

日本の労働人口は約6300万人で、そのうち4分の1はサービス業に従事している。

日本人の収入

日本の労働者の平均的な世帯収入は1カ月約53万円。支出は約33万円。

1 Japanese Government

❑ Cabinet and Diet

Q How is the government set up in Japan?

The Japanese government is similar to the governments of other developed countries with separation of power. There are three branches of political power: the legislative power, held by the National Diet; the executive power, held by the Cabinet; and the judicial power, held by the courts.

The National Diet is divided into two houses —the House of Representatives and the House of Councilors. The members of the two houses are elected by the people. The prime minister is chosen by the Diet.

The 11 ministries in the Cabinet are:
- Cabinet Office
- Ministry of Internal Affairs and Communications

- Ministry of Justice
- Ministry of Foreign Affairs
- Ministry of Finance
- Ministry of Education, Culture, Sports, Science and Technology
- Ministry of Health, Labour and Welfare
- Ministry of Agriculture, Forestry and Fisheries
- Ministry of Economy, Trade and Industry
- Ministry of Land, Infrastructure and Transport
- Ministry of the Environment

The ministers can be either private citizens or government officials. It is also common for scholars to be chosen as ministers. In the past, there have been only two or three women in the Cabinet. But now women are being chosen for more important ministries, including the Ministry of Foreign Affairs.

Q When was the legislature created?

Japan's first legislature was the Imperial Diet set up by the Meiji Constitution. It lasted from 1889 to 1947. The Meiji Constitution was adopted on February 11,

1889, and the Imperial Diet first met on November 29, 1890. The Diet consisted of a House of Representatives and a House of Peers. The House of Representatives was directly elected by the people. Starting in 1925, all adult males had the right to vote. The House of Peers was like the British House of Lords, and the members were high-ranking nobles.

The Constitution of Japan, adopted in 1947, was a more democratic system. The name was changed from the Imperial Diet to the National Diet. Under the new Constitution, women could vote for the first time. The House of Peers was abolished and replaced with the directly elected House of Councilors. The powers of the emperor were also restricted.

Q What is the Diet?

The National Diet of Japan is Japan's legislature. There are two houses: the House of Representatives and the House of Councilors.

Both houses of the Diet are directly elected under a parallel voting system. The National Diet Building is located in Nagatacho, Chiyoda Ward, Tokyo.

It is the job of the Diet to pass laws and also to select the prime minister. It also ratifies treaties, approves the budget, proposes amendments to the constitution and investigates government activities.

In America, when people want to talk about the government, they often just say "Washington." In Japan, the word that often refers to the national government is "Nagatacho." When Japanese say "Nagatacho," that often means the Diet or the Diet members.

After living in Tokyo for many years, one day I decided to visit Nagatacho. You have to make an appointment to go inside the Diet, but it is interesting to just walk around and see all the big and historical buildings. There are a lot of police and guards along the streets, so try not to act too suspicious!

Q How many members of the Diet are there?

The Constitution of Japan does not cover such topics as the number of members of each house of the Diet, the voting system, and the qualifications for voting. All of these things are decided by law.

There are 480 members in the House of Representatives, and in the House of Councilors there are 242 members who serve for 6 years. The Constitution of Japan guarantees the right to vote and a secret ballot. It also says that the election law must be fair concerning "race, creed, sex, social status, family origin, education, property or income."

❑ Elections

Q How does the election system work?

Both houses of the Diet are elected under a parallel voting system. The seats to be filled are divided into two groups. Each group is elected by a different method. Voters are asked to cast two votes: one for an individual candidate, and one for a party list.

Of the 480 members of the House of Representatives, 300 are elected from the districts. And 180 are elected from 11 separate electoral blocks under the party list system of proportional representation.

Of the 242 members of the House of Councilors, 146 are elected from 47 prefectures. The remaining 96 are elected by a nation-wide proportional representation system.

Q What percentage of the voters vote?

The voting rate in the rural areas of Japan is higher than 50%. But in the cities the rate is usually far less than 50%, although about 30% of the people in Japan live in big cities. It seems that people are losing interest in politics.

One morning when I first came to Japan, I was suddenly woken up by a loudspeaker outside my window. I didn't know what was happening. Later, I learned that an election was coming up and the politicians were driving around in their campaign cars shouting. They mostly just shouted their names and said, "Please vote for me!"

It seems that when people vote in Japan they don't know very much about what the politicians really think. There are no debates, and few people talk about policy. Political parties sometimes tell voters about the policies of the party. But politicians very seldom tell people what they personally think. I guess in Japan the political parties have a lot of power and individual politicians have almost none.

❏ Political Issues

Q Who has the most political power in Japan?

In America and other countries, there are two strong political parties, but in Japan the Liberal Democratic Party has more power than any other party in the country. Since 1945, all of the prime ministers, except for four, were from the Liberal Democratic Party. It has been the strongest party in Japanese politics for more than 50 years. The other major party is the Democratic Party of Japan. But, as of now, the Liberal Democratic Party is the strongest party in Japan.

Q Do people talk about politics much in Japan?

No, they don't. In America, Europe and other countries, it seems that people often talk about politics. They sometimes even get in fights about politics. But in Japan it seems that people don't talk about politics very much at all. I first thought that they didn't talk to me about Japanese politics because I was a foreigner. But now I know that they don't talk to each other very much about politics. I guess this is because Japanese want to maintain harmony.

But in recent years there have been more debate programs on TV about politics. So I think it is becoming a little easier for Japanese to talk about politics with each other.

Q What are the main problems faced by the government?

Up until the early 1990s, the economy in Japan was very strong. Everyone seemed to be happy, and it seemed like there weren't any really big problems. But by the middle of the 1990s, the economy was not so strong. People were not happy with the government and it seemed like there were many problems to deal with. The government faced a lot of challenges in reforming the banking, postal, and education systems.

Q Are politicians involved in many scandals?

When I first came to Japan, it seemed like there were almost no scandals. In fact, it seemed like there were almost no problems in Japan at all. I'm sure politicians and other people with power did bad things, but not very many were investigated or arrested. And the media also seemed to keep very quiet about scandals.

But now it seems like every time you turn on the TV or read a newspaper, you hear about a new scandal. Some people think that Japan is becoming more corrupt. But I think that there are just more people getting caught and the media no longer hesitates to report such corruption.

One of the reasons for this is that Japan's press is quite free. In fact, it can be said that many of the reforms taking place in Japan are being pushed by the media. The main duty of the media is to be a watchdog over government, and it seems that the media in Japan is doing a much better job in recent years.

❑ Diplomacy

Q Does Japan have good relationships with other countries?

Before and during World War II, Japan tried to take over other countries in Asia. As a result of this, many people in those countries do not think very well of Japan. But it looks like the situation is getting better. Japan has tried hard to make friends and gives a lot of money to other countries through ODA. This has helped to improve relationships with other countries.

There has also been a big improvement in the relationship between Japan and South Korea. The two cultures are very close to each other in some ways. Many Japanese like Korean movie stars and more and more people are trying to learn Korean. For the Japanese, Korean is probably easier to learn than English.

On the other hand, Japan is still having difficulty with some neighbors. The relationship with China is especially sensitive. To Japanese, it seems that China focuses a lot on Japan's crimes during World War II. The Chinese don't feel that Japan fully understands the pain that it has caused China. However, Japan and China are doing a lot of trading with each other. Many Japanese manufacturers have set up factories in China. Japan also shares a lot of technology with China. It can be said that the relationship with China is improving slowly.

Q What is the relationship between Japan and North Korea like?

North Korea admits that it kidnapped some Japanese people several years ago. Some of them have returned safely to Japan. But most Japanese think that North Korea kidnapped many more people, and Japan should not help North Korea in any way until this problem is cleared up. It is also thought that North Korea has nuclear weapons. So some people think that Japan must not make North Korea angry. In any case, it is a complicated problem and no one knows what will happen in the future.

Before coming to Japan, I thought that Asian countries were mostly friendly with each other. Most foreigners don't understand how different Asian countries are. To many people from Europe and America, the language, traditional music, food, and culture all seem similar. They also think that Asian people all think alike.

It is true that there haven't been very many wars in recent years. But most countries in Asia have fought with each other at some time in history. They have very different ways of thinking. In Europe, countries work closely with each other under the European Union. In North America, there is NAFTA and many other trade agreements. But in Asia, there are not many close trade agreements. It does seem that Asia is getting closer together, but there is still a long way to go. Most foreigners don't realize how complicated Asia is.

Q: Does Japan get along well with the United States?

Everyone knows that Japan lost World War II to the United States and its allies. But after the war, America helped Japan reconstruct the country and won the respect of the Japanese people.

Of course, American culture is also very popular in Japan. To some people, it seems like Japan is closer to America than to Asia. This is especially true when talking about the economy. It is said that when America catches a cold, Japan sneezes!

But the young people of today do not know much about the war. They are becoming more independent. They are less likely to accept America's world leadership than older people in Japan. It sometimes seems that America makes Japan do things that the people really don't want to do. Especially with economic issues and military affairs, Japan will probably not follow America so closely in the future.

2 Japanese Economy

❑ Economic Issues

Q Why is Japan's economy so strong?

Everyone in the world knows that Japanese work hard and also study hard. These two things help to make Japan's economy strong.

But some people are worried about the future of Japan. Young people in Japan do not seem so interested in studying and working hard.

For about 30 years, real economic growth was very strong. It was 10% a year in the 1960s, then 5% in the 1970s, and 4% in the 1980s. But in the 1990s, growth slowed to only 1.7%. This was mostly because of the "economic bubble" during the late 1980s. The government has tried many things to improve the economy, but the recovery has been slow.

Q What are the biggest problems that the government needs to take care of?

Japan now has a very big debt: it is more than 150% of the GDP. Japan's population is getting older. Japan's elderly population (65 or older) is the biggest of all industrialized countries, and the birthrate is the lowest. In order to take care of all these old people, more money will be needed. But there are not enough young people to support the current pension system. The government is trying to raise taxes, but some people think this will hurt the economy even more. The economy in Japan is strong now, but if something is not done soon, the country will not be able to stay strong.

Q Who are the people on Japanese bills?

In November 2004, Japan issued bills with new designs for the first time in 20 years. It is hoped that it will not be possible to copy the new money. The ¥1,000 bill has a picture of Hideyo Noguchi on it. He was a famous Japanese medical reseracher. The ¥5,000 bill has a picture of Ichiyo Higuchi, an author in the

Meiji era and the first woman to appear on Japanese money. The ¥10,000 bill has Yukichi Fukuzawa on it. He was an educator in the Meiji Period.

When I first went to a bank in Japan, I was very surprised. I couldn't believe how fast people counted money. They spread out the bills and count them very quickly. In America, people usually count money one bill at a time. So it takes a lot of time to count large amounts of money. Now in Japan most banks use counting machines, and you don't see people count money by hand very much anymore.

❏ Trading

Q Does Japan export a lot of products?

Japan makes a lot of products and sells them to other countries. The major products are cars, computers, and technology. About 25% of the products that Japan makes are sold to the United States. And about one third of Japan's exports go to Asia.

Japan exports more than it imports. This is because Japan imports a lot of raw materials and then it makes products to send to other countries. Japan is known around the world for its high-quality electronic equipment. Japan also exports a lot of advanced technology.

Q What kinds of things does Japan import?

About 60% of Japan's food is imported. There is not very much land for farming in Japan. The country also imports almost 100% of its oil. If Japan could not import those items, it would be a big problem for everyday life.

The Japanese economy depends strongly on trading, and the location of Japan makes success possible. All areas of Japan are close to the ocean and sending things from Japan to California is easier than sending things from New York to California.

3 Social Issues in Japan

❑ Crime

Q Is Japan a safe country?

Japan has a very low crime rate. Since World War II, the crime rate has dropped. This has not happened in any other country in the world. You can walk on the street at night, even in Tokyo and Osaka. Japanese usually feel safe in their homes and when they go out. Even the most dangerous parts of the big cities are not very dangerous.

When Japanese go to other countries, they are often the victims of crime. This is probably because Japanese aren't used to thinking about crime in their daily lives.

I remember a few years ago sitting on a crowded train and watching a Japanese man not far from me counting his money. He probably had ¥2,000,000 and he didn't seem worried at all. I would never show strangers so much money, but I'm quite sure that man made it home safely. Although crime is increasing in Japan, it is still a very safe country.

Q Has the crime rate in Japan gone up recently?

Yes. For many years, Japanese felt very safe, but many Japanese are feeling less safe now. In the news, you can often hear about very bad crimes. The crime rate has gone up since the late 1990s, and many people feel that it will get worse.

A study in Tokyo in 2003 showed that over 19% of all people in Tokyo had experienced a crime. In 1993, the number of cases reported to the police in Japan was 1,801,150 and there were 723,610 arrests. By 2003, the number of reported cases was 2,790,136 and the number of arrests was 648,319. The number of arrests dropped in the 10-year period. So people do not feel as safe as they did a few years ago.

Some people think that the crime rate and the economy are related. If the economy goes down, crime will increase. When people don't have jobs or hope of finding jobs, they are more likely to do something illegal. The crime rate by young people is also going up and up.

Q What is being done to cut crime?

Japan has a lot of police officers. In fact, there are more officers in Japan than in most other countries. But the country is planning to increase the number of police officers. New technology is also being used to help lower crime.

There are many *koban* police boxes, but they are often empty. Sometimes if you call the police, it takes a long time for them to get there.

❏ Changes in the Family

Q Why is the birthrate falling?

Japan now has one of the lowest birthrates of any developed country. The government knows that if the population decreases, it will hurt the economy in the long run. Taxes will need to be increased so that fewer workers can help support the older population. This is not an easy problem to solve. There are many issues that need to be thought about.

Many people feel that to have more than one or two children is too expensive. It is expensive to raise a child in Japan. Parents usually have to spend a lot of money on tuition for *juku* (cram schools) to help get their children into college.

Another issue is that fewer people are getting married. Many men and women would like to get married, but many others feel that they can live happily without getting married. No one seems to know what to do to solve this very serious problem.

And if you live in a city and don't have a car, it can be very difficult to get around with young children. I remember walking down a sidewalk along a busy street. I saw a mother with three young children walking ahead of me. A car suddenly turned off the road onto the sidewalk and almost hit one of the children. The mother got really angry and started screaming at the driver and hitting his car with her hands. I had never seen anything like it! Most Japanese do not get angry in public so easily, but I also understand how the mother felt. Most sidewalks in Japan are not very wide and they are very close to busy streets. It's one more reason why taking care of young children in Japan is difficult.

Q Are elderly people well taken care of?

The Japanese have a long average lifespan. This is probably because they have a healthy diet and take care of their health. But because the population is getting older, there are some special problems that Japan needs to deal with. One problem is that there are fewer people to work and pay taxes. At the same time, there are more people to be taken care of. As a result, Japan is raising its consumption tax. But many people still do not feel secure about their future. They fear that they won't be able to take care of themselves in their old age, and the government won't be able to help them, either.

Q Is it easy for women to get work?

For many years in Japan, very few women had full-time jobs. But this has changed in recent years. More and more women want to work and not have a family, or they want to have a family and continue working. It is probably much easier for a woman to work in Japan now than it was 10 or 20 years ago.

But the workplace does not seem equal in every way. Less than 1% of the board directors of Japanese companies listed on the Tokyo Stock Exchange are women.

It is clear, however, that many Japanese companies have been able to succeed by using the skills of women. In fact, it is thought that many companies could do better if they hired the best person for the job, instead of hiring mostly men.

Share of Women in the Labor Force (2003)

	(%)
United States	59.5
Britain	55.3
Germany	49.3
France	49.2
Japan	48.3

source: Ministry of Internal Affairs and Communications

❑ Foreigners in Japan

Q Are there many foreigners in Japan?

There are now more foreigners in Japan than ever before. Koreans and Chinese make up the biggest groups and the Brazilians come next. Many Japanese emigrated to Brazil. Now, their descendants are coming back. About 47,000 people from the U.S. are living in Japan.

Unfortunately, there are many illegal foreigners and the government is trying to lower the number.

Q Do Japanese welcome foreigners?

Japan doesn't accept a lot of immigrants and it is a rather closed society compared to other developed countries. Some people are afraid of having a lot of foreign residents because they might change the current society. But the population is getting older and Japan may need to find new workers from foreign countries to keep the economy strong.

There are other reasons that Japanese are likely

to keep away from foreigners. If you are a foreigner and sit on a train in Japan, you will probably notice that sometimes Japanese don't sit next to you. Even if the train is crowded, sometimes people will still not sit next to you. You might think that this is because Japanese don't like foreigners. But this is probably not the case.

Many Japanese feel that they should speak English but can't. If they sit next to a foreigner, they are afraid that you might ask them something and they won't be able to reply. In order to avoid such an embarrassing situation, many Japanese try to stay away from foreigners. But many Japanese are very friendly, even if they are not confident in their English skills, and are willing to talk to foreigners.

4 Japanese at Work

❏ Labor Conditions

Weekly Working Hours (2002)	(Hours)
Britain	41.0
United States	40.9
France	35.3
Germany	37.6
Japan	37.8

Unemployment Rate (2002)	(%)
France	8.9
Germany	8.7
United States	5.8
Japan	5.4
Britain	5.1

source: Ministry of Internal Affairs and Communications

Q Is the labor force changing?

Japanese workers usually work long hours. It is said that they do this because they like their companies. Companies have traditionally taken care of their workers for life. People could work at the same company as long as they wanted to. But this is changing. More and more workers want to have free time. And some young people don't want to work for a company at all, so they just work part time.

And in recent years, however, the economy hasn't been so strong, so this is changing little by little. Companies make their staff work harder now and only want to keep the good workers. Many people have had to change jobs.

Q What industries have the most workers in Japan?

There are about 63 million workers in Japan. One quarter of all workers work in the service industries. About 23% work in the wholesale, retail and restaurant businesses, and about 19% work in manufacturing. In 1960, about 30% of all workers worked on farms, but now the figure is less than 5%.

Q What is the unemployment rate in Japan?

Since World War II, the unemployment rate has

been mostly between 1% and 2%. But the economy has been weak for many years now, and so the rate is currently about 5%. This is lower than in European countries, but for Japan this seems very high.

Q Is it difficult to find a job?

Right now, it is hard to find a good job in Japan. Many people, especially young and old people, can't find work. But in the future there will not be enough workers. Japan's population is getting older and women are having fewer children. From around 2007, it is predicted that the number of workers in Japan will start to fall.

Q How many days do Japanese have off a year?

About 60% of workers in Japan have 2 days off a week. This is much more than in the past. There are 15 national holidays each year. Many workers also have 8 days off in the summer and 4 to 6 days off over New

Year. Workers also have about 18 days of annual leave each year, but most workers only take about 10 days off. The average worker in Japan has 120 days off a year.

❑ Customs in the Workplace

Q **What is it like to work for a Japanese company?**

When you go into a Japanese company, the first thing you will see is that there are almost no private offices. Most workers just have a desk and sit very close to each other. Even company managers often don't have their own office. Many offices are open with no dividing walls between the desks. Part of the reason for this is because office space costs a lot of money in Japan.

Japanese also like to make sure there is smooth communication between staff. Having no walls seems to make it easier to talk with other workers in the company.

Q What is a *salaryman*?

In the West, the company you work for is not so important. Your own career is more important. If someone asks a person from the West, "What do you do?" they will probably say something like, "I'm an accountant," or "I'm an engineer." But Japanese give the name of the company they work for. Or say something like "I'm a *salaryman*." For Japanese, the company seems to be more important than their own career. Right now, about 70% of students become *salaryman* when they graduate from college.

Q What do people wear to work?

In the West, it is common now for office workers to wear casual clothes to work. But in Japan, it is still common to wear a suit, white shirt and a tie. Some companies are starting to change, but if you get on a train during the rush hour, you will see that most businessmen still wear dark business suits. It is like a uniform for *salaryman*.

It seems to me that Japanese like to wear uniforms. Many students and also people who work in factories often wear uniforms. But even female office workers often wear uniforms to work. They would feel embarrassed riding home on the trains in their uniforms, so they get to work early to change their clothes.

Q What about lunch breaks?

In most companies in Japan, the lunch break is very short and many people eat at their desk. Lunch is not a time to talk or to eat with a client. In the past, it was common for people to take *bento* (boxed lunches) to work, but now most people usually get lunch at a convenience store or eat out.

Q Is there a lot of overtime work?

In Japan, it is not unusual for workers to stay at their desk for several hours in the evening. Japanese workers often feel bad about going home before their boss or other people. Most people don't want to be the first person in their office to go home. Some people say that they can get more work done when most of the other workers have already gone. There has recently been some concern about the stress that office workers have in their 40s and 50s. There are about 10,000 *karoshi* (deaths from overwork) every year.

Q Is smoking allowed in offices?

Up until about 10 years ago, Japan was a difficult place to live and work for non-smokers. I remember going to meetings and restaurants and the entire room would be filled with smoke. In one office where I worked, we got new computers, but within a few months, all the computers were brown because of the smoke.

But the situation has been changing, and now in many offices smoking is prohibited.

I personally don't smoke, so I'm happy with the change. But many of my friends do smoke. They often complain how difficult it has become for them. Most offices ban smoking, and so do many restaurants and coffee shops. And in some parts of Japan, it is even against the law to smoke as you walk along the street. Japan is no longer a smoker's paradise.

Q Why are business cards so important in Japan?

In the West, business cards are not so important. They are just pieces of paper with contact information—nothing more. But in Japan business cards are one of the most important tools that a business person has. In the West, business cards are most often given at the end of a meeting so that people will know how to contact each other. But in Japan, business cards are always given at the beginning of a meeting when people meet for the first time.

How you talk to the other person often depends on the company and their position in the company. If you don't have a business card, then people might think that you are not very important and they might not treat you very well.

Q Do co-workers often go drinking together?

In a Japanese company, it is very important to get along well with the other workers. It is not so easy to change jobs in Japan, so you don't want to make enemies with people you may have to work with for many years. If you go drinking with your co-workers, you might be able to talk about problems and work them out. If you don't go drinking, the workers who do go might talk about you behind your back!

❑ Income and spending

Q How much do Japanese make and how much do they spend?

The average worker-household in Japan earns about ¥530,000 per month. In the last few years, the average income has been dropping because the economy is still weak and the unemployment rate is increasing. There are also more people working in lower-paid service industries and more part-time workers.

The average household in Japan spends about ¥330,000 per month. This has also been dropping in recent years.

Q How do Japanese spend their money?

About 25% of the money that Japanese spend goes to food, which is less than in the U.S. but almost the same as European countries. On the other hand, Japanese spend 14% on education and entertainment, which is rather higher than other countries. This may prove how interested they are in their children's education.

Monthly Income and Spending

(Yen)

	2001	2002	2003	2004
Income	551,160	538,277	524,542	530,028
Disposable income	464,723	452,501	440,461	444,966
Living expenditures	335,042	330,651	325,823	330,836

source: Ministry of Internal Affairs and Communications

5 Japanese in School

❑ Education System

Q What is the education system like?

Japan uses the "6-3-3-4" education system, which is the same as in the United States. This means that there are six years of elementary school, three years of middle school, three years of high school, and four years at a university. This system was set up by the School Education Law in 1947.

Elementary school and three years of middle school are compulsory. Most children also go to nursery school and kindergarten. About 95% of middle school graduates go on to high school. And about 50% of high school graduates go on to a two-year college, a four-year college or a university.

Q Why do many students go to cram schools?

In Japan, almost anyone can go to high school and college. But to enter a good high school or university, students need to pass difficult exams. They go to *juku* cram schools so that they can pass these difficult exams. About 50% of 5th and 6th grade students go to private *juku* for extra schooling after regular school.

In Japan, if you go to a good high school and university, you can usually find a good job. It will influence the rest of your life.

But now there are not as many children and students as in the past. Many people don't think that the tests to get into a good school should be hard. It is likely that the education system will change slowly in the coming years.

Q Is it true that it is difficult to get into a university but easy to graduate?

The exams to get into a good school or university in Japan are very difficult. Students have to study very hard day and night to be able to pass.

But when they do pass, it is like joining a club. The school feels like they have to help all the students who get into the school to graduate. Of course, in some universities you have to study very hard so that you can graduate. But at many universities, you do not have to study very hard and you can still graduate.

Q Are most people happy with the education system as it is now?

In the past, it seemed that most people were happy with the education system. But now it does not have such a good reputation. Several years ago, the Japanese government changed its thinking and tried to make changes. It wanted to make the education system more relaxed.

But now, when Japan's education level is compared with the levels of other countries, a fall in achievement levels can be seen. According to a survey by the Organization for Economic Cooperation and Development, Japanese students were 6th in math literacy and 14th in reading among 38 other countries in 2003. In the previous survey in 2000, Japan was 1st in math and 8th in reading. The government is now trying to change this and go back to a system that requires students to study harder.

Q Can foreigners go to a Japanese university?

Most of the universities in Japan welcome students from other countries. To get into some universities, you will need to take some exams. You might also have to take a *kanji* test, but at some universities you do not need to know Japanese.

There were about 2.8 million university students in 2004. Of this total, 117,302 were students from foreign countries. More students come from China (77,713) than any other country, followed by Korea and Taiwan.

I have an American friend who came to Tokyo to study Japanese at a university. He met another exchange student there from Korea and they fell in love and got married. They still live in Japan, but their children speak Japanese, Korean, and English. Japan is becoming more international all the time.

Q Do Japanese children learn English at school?

During the nine years of compulsory education, all children learn English. And some students also go on home-stay holidays during the summer to improve their English. Many university students learn English as part of their basic education, and so it is common for Japanese to study English for about eight years. Still, most people in Japan feel that they can't speak English.

Q Many Japanese seem to be able to read English, but they can't speak it well. Why is this?

Most lessons in schools are taught by Japanese teachers and students learn mainly reading and grammar. But recently this is changing. More and more schools are employing native assistant teachers to work along with the Japanese English teachers to help the students learn to speak natural English.

Not long after coming to Japan for the first time, a man told me that he spoke better English when he was drunk. I didn't think this was true. But after being in Japan for a few years, I started to think it was true. There are probably many reasons why Japanese have difficulty with English, but maybe one of the biggest reasons is that they worry about making mistakes. When they get a little drunk, they don't seem to worry so much about mistakes. Of course, it probably won't help to get really drunk!

Q Many Japanese take English exams. Why doesn't this improve their speaking skills?

The most popular English exams in Japan are TOEIC, TOEFL and EIKEN. People usually take these tests so they can go to an American university or get a promotion at work. Most exams only test grammar, vocabulary, reading and listening skills. You don't have to be able to speak English to get a high score.

So many Japanese can do quite well on the tests, but still they may not be able to speak English well. For many it is difficult to speak a foreign language because they are too shy or because they get embarrassed easily.

My parents once came to Japan for a visit. I decided to invite a friend of mine who taught English in high school to go to a restaurant with us. My parents looked forward to meeting someone they could talk with in English. But I'm afraid the English teacher could hardly say anything. Later, I told my parents that the teacher could probably answer any question about grammar, but he still couldn't have a simple conversation in English. The Japanese are getting better at English, but foreigners are always surprised to meet people who can teach English, but not speak it.

Q: Is anything being done to improve the English-language ability of the Japanese?

In recent years, many schools have started employing native teachers to teach English conversation in public schools, but often the teacher's Japanese seems to improve more quickly than the students' English!

Another way that students can improve their English is to go to a private English-conversation school, although this can cost a lot of money.

There are many radio and TV programs and also

books to help people learn English. Bookstores are filled with these kinds of books, and in fact, Japan might be one of the best places to learn English!

Part 3

Japanese Life and Culture

読みはじめる前に

Part 3 で使われている用語です。わからない語は巻末のワードリストで確認しましょう。

- [ ] ceremony
- [ ] custom
- [ ] expense
- [ ] festival
- [ ] household
- [ ] ingredient
- [ ] landlord
- [ ] leisure
- [ ] religion
- [ ] rent
- [ ] shrine
- [ ] temple
- [ ] theater
- [ ] tradition

知っておきたい基本情報

物価指数
ニューヨークを100とすると、東京は134.7、大阪は121.8。物価の面からすると、日本の都市は、外国人にとって暮らしやすいとは言えない。

日本人の結婚
日本人の結婚のうち13％はお見合いと、まだまだ多い。合コンも現代のお見合いと言えるかもしれない。

日本の名所
日本三景と呼ばれるのは「天橋立」(京都)、「宮島」(広島)、「松島」(宮城)。富士山の高さは3776m、最近世界遺産に指定されたのは「紀伊山地の霊場と参詣道」など。

日本の祭り
東京の三大祭は「山王祭」「三社祭」「神田祭」。ほかの有名な祭りは、「さっぽろ雪まつり」(北海道)、「祇園祭」(京都)、「仙台七夕祭り」(宮城)など。

日本の伝統芸能
歌舞伎は16世紀に、出雲阿国という女性が始めた。茶道もやはり16世紀に、千利休によって完成された。

1 Japanese at Home

❏ Cities

Q What are the most populous cities in Japan?

A large majority of Japanese people live in urban areas. About 27% of the population lives in Tokyo and the surrounding prefectures.

Tokyo is the most populous city, with about 12 million people. This is followed by Yokohama, Osaka and Nagoya, all west of Tokyo and on the island of Honshu.

When talking about Tokyo, the city is sometimes divided into two parts: *Shitamachi* and *Yamanote*. *Shitamachi* means "lower town." It refers to the low parts of Tokyo on the east side. This is where traditional working-class neighborhoods can be found. *Yamanote* means "mountain hand." It is the part of the midtown area where the samurai and lords lived in the Edo Period.

Q Is Japan covered in urban areas?

It is easy to think that most of Japan is covered in buildings and roads. But there are still a lot of rural and wildlife areas in Japan. If you take a one-hour train ride out of Tokyo, you will find yourself in the countryside. There are many forests and mountains. You can also still find villages where people choose to live a simple and slow life. Many foreigners who live in Japan choose to live in such areas, where they can enjoy a more traditional way of Japanese life.

❑ Housing

Q Are Japanese homes small?

If you are new to Japan, then you will probably think that Japanese homes are very small. In the big cities, most people live in small apartments. The average size of a house or apartment for all of Japan is 1,023 square feet (about 95 square meters).

In Tokyo, there is not very much land and so prices are very high. Most Japanese do not take visitors home because their houses are packed with personal items and they don't think they have enough space to invite guests.

Japanese homes are not only small, the ceilings and doorways are often not very high. I have an American friend who is a little tall. I met him after he moved into an apartment and he had two or three bruises on his head. When I asked him what happened, he said that he kept hitting his head on the doorways. Fortunately, this is not a problem I have had to worry about.

Q Why don't people move away from the big cities so they can live in bigger houses or apartments?

Most of the jobs in Japan are in the big cities. Some people do work in the city and live in the country, commuting to work by train. Many workers in Tokyo take one and a half hours or longer to travel to work and some people use the Shinkansen "bullet train" to go to work.

❏ Japanese homes

Q When I go into a Japanese home, where do I take my shoes off?

As soon as you enter a house in Japan, you will see a *genkan* entrance hall. This is where you need to take off your shoes. There will be slippers waiting for you. You can wear slippers in the rooms with flooring or carpet, but don't wear them on tatami mats.

When you first put on slippers, you may not like them at first. But if you are visiting someone's home, you are expected to wear them.

There are special slippers for the bathroom. Make sure you don't wear them outside the bathroom.

Q What are Japanese toilets like?

Most homes now have Western-style toilets, but some homes still have Japanese-style ones. These toilets do not have a place for you to sit. Instead, you squat over the top of the toilet. Some people think they are difficult to use, but other people like them better because they think they are easier and cleaner.

Q What are Japanese baths like?

Most Japanese baths are square and deep. Before you get in the bath, you need to wash your body. When you are clean, you can get in the hot water and sit for several minutes.

Other people might use the same hot water after you. You might not like Japanese-style baths at first. But most people start to really like them after a while. In some homes, the same bath water is reheated so that it can be used again.

Q What are tatami?

Tatami mats are made of straw. If the tatami is new, it feels and smells very nice. Most people change the tatami every four or five years. In Japan, when telling someone how big a room is, the number of tatami mats is often used. So you might say that your bedroom is a "4-mat" or a "6-mat" room.

Japan FAQ

Q Do most people in Japan use futon?

Some people have beds, but more people have futon. If you sleep on a futon mattress, you should put it away every morning. Japanese like futon because they don't take up very much space.

Q Is it true that Japanese homes have paper doors and windows?

Yes. *Shoji* are sliding doors made of wood and paper. *Fusuma* are like doors with paper on both sides. *Shoji* and *fusuma* can be removed to make one large room.

Q What heating is used in the winter?

In the parts of Japan where it is cold, most people have kerosene or gas stoves. Many homes also have a *kotatsu*. This is a low table with an electric heater underneath. A blanket is put over the top to keep the heat in. When it is really cold, a *kotatsu* feels very nice and warm. Most modern buildings have full air-conditioning.

Q What is a *butsudan*?

A *butsudan* is a Buddhist altar for praying to family members who have died. It is often decorated with candles and food offerings and is a special place in Japanese homes. Some homes also have a Shinto *kamidana*, where family members pray for safety and prosperity. The *kamidana* altar is decorated with rice and *sake*.

Q Do all Japanese homes have a *tokonoma*?

In the past, they did. A *tokonoma* is an alcove the size of half a tatami mat or one tatami mat. It is usually decorated with a hanging scroll and a flower arrangement. Nowadays, many new homes don't have *tokonoma*, because they take up space that can be used for other things. But traditionally this is also a special place in

Japanese homes. You shouldn't sit in the *tokonoma* or put your things there.

Q What should you do if you are invited to a Japanese home?

Most people do not invite people, even close friends, to come into their homes or to stay over, as is done in the West. It is more common for them to take you out to a restaurant.

If you do go to a Japanese home, you should try to be on time—neither early nor late. It's always a good idea to take a simple gift. Some cookies or a bottle of wine will be fine. But your hosts probably won't open the gift in front of you.

Usually the wife will be very busy serving you drinks and food. You might ask her to relax, but it probably won't slow her down.

❑ Living expenses

Q Does it cost a lot to live in Japan?

Japanese have the 6th highest average income in the world, but it costs more to live in Tokyo than any other city in the world. If the cost of living in New York City is 100 on an index, Tokyo is 134.7 and Osaka is 121.8.

The average household spends 17.9% of its income on food, about 4% each on education, utilities and clothes, and 8.1% on culture and entertainment. But if you want to save money, you can. There are many discount stores in Japan. And you can even get your hair cut for as little as ¥1,000.

Q How about apartments?

The size of a Japanese apartment is usually given in the number of rooms. For example, 1R refers to a one-room apartment with a bathroom. A 2LDK refers to a two-bedroom apartment with a living/dining room, a bathroom, and a kitchen.

A one-bedroom apartment with living/dining room, a bathroom and a kitchen (1LDK) will be about ¥80,000 to ¥100,000 in Tokyo. But if you want to live close to a train station or in a really nice area, it will cost more.

Q How much does it cost to move into a new apartment?

You need to pay about five months' rent before you move into a new apartment: one month's rent; two months' worth of *shikikin* and one month's worth of *reikin*; and one month's worth of commission. You might also have to pay a maintenance fee and insurance.

Shikikin is a deposit paid to the owner or landlord. When you move out, it is used to pay for rent you haven't paid or to pay for cleaning and any repairs necessary after you move out. It will be returned to you if you pay your rent and take good care of the apartment.

Reikin is a fee that you pay to the owner of the apartment to say thank you for letting you rent the room and it will not be given back to you when you move out.

Q Is food expensive in Japan?

Japan imports about 60% of its food. Imported items are mainly fish, meat, corn, wheat and coffee. Japan has little control over the price of imported products.

Most of the staples of the Japanese diet are produced in the country, including 92% of rice, 98% of eggs, 88% of vegetables, 67% of meat, and 66% of fish and shellfish.

The average household of 3.5 people spends an average of ¥78,059 (17.9% of income) per month on food. Because of the intense competition between the fast-food chains, prices are cheaper in Japan than in many other countries.

Interestingly, despite the imbalance between Japan's food imports and exports, Japanese foods such as sushi, tofu, and green tea have become very popular overseas in recent years.

2 Japanese Ceremonies

❑ Marriage

Q Are many Japanese marriages still arranged?

Traditionally, marriages were an arrangement between families, rather than individuals. But since 1995, only 13% of marriages are *omiai* (arranged marriages) and 87% are love marriages.

With an *omiai* marriage, a matchmaker exchanges photographs and self-introduction notes between a man and a woman. If they are interested in each other, the matchmaker arranges a meeting, usually in a hotel or restaurant.

Although *omiai* marriages arranged by parents are decreasing, a lot of people still meet at *gokon* parties, which are held to bring potential couples together.

Q How do people get married in Japan?

In Japan, there are many types of marriage ceremonies. To make your marriage official, all you need to do is go to the city hall where you live and register.

But most people have some type of ceremony, big or small. A Shinto wedding is the most expensive. It costs a lot of money for the ceremony, including a fee for using the shrine, renting the kimonos (the bride usually changes costume several times), and the reception party for the guests.

Western-style ceremonies are becoming more popular. It is said that about two-thirds of all the wedding ceremonies in Japan are now Western-style.

Q How do couples pay for the wedding?

Some couples save money for their marriage and some ask their parents to pay. But *oiwai-kin* also helps cover the cost of a wedding. *Oiwai-kin* is a cash gift you should give if you are invited as a guest to a wedding in Japan. The typical amount is ¥20,000 or ¥30,000. But the amount will be more if you are a relative or the boss of the bride or bridegroom.

The couple usually uses half this money to pay for the wedding and returns half to the guest in the form of a gift. You should give the money in a special envelope decorated with red and white or silver and gold string.

Q What part does religion play in Japanese weddings?

When Westerners get married in a church wedding, they usually exchange their vows before God. In Japan, weddings can be held at a Christian church or a Shinto shrine. But for most couples it's a matter of style and not a matter of religion. Japanese usually don't think very much about religion when getting married, or when getting divorced.

❑ Funerals

Q What are funerals like in Japan?

Funerals in Japan are usually Buddhist. It is not

unusual for a person to have a Shinto wedding and a Buddhist funeral. Bodies are cremated, and then the ashes are put in a family grave at a Buddhist temple.

It is the responsibility of the oldest son in Japan to take care of the family grave. But many people think that the cost of a funeral is too high. The average grave in Japan costs about ¥2.5 million, including the land-use fee and the price of a gravestone. Today, other types of funeral are becoming more common.

I had an American friend who said that she bought a beautiful bouquet of colorful flowers to take to a Japanese funeral. When she arrived, she realized that all the other flowers were white. The family was very polite, and they put her colorful flowers next to the white flowers. But she said that she was quite embarrassed because her flowers stuck out so much.

3 Japanese Food

❑ Ingredients

Q: Is rice the most common ingredient of Japanese meals?

Yes. Almost all meals in Japan come with rice. There are usually side dishes that you eat with rice.

Rice is thought to be almost sacred and is still used in some ceremonies. Until the end of the Edo Period (1867), Buddhists in Japan did not eat meat. Instead, rice was used in many different ways: to make desserts, snacks, vinegar and *sake*.

When you eat Japanese food, you should try to finish the rice and the side dishes at about the same time. You can always tell when someone is not used to eating Japanese food because they either have a lot of rice left after eating their side dishes or a lot of side dishes left after eating their rice.

Sushi is the most popular rice dish. Most sushi is made with a small handful of rice and is topped with a small piece of seafood (raw or cooked), vegetable, or egg. *Kaitenzushi* shops, where the plates of sushi go around on a conveyor belt are common.

You can also have a bowl of rice with *sashimi* (raw fish) on top of it.

Onigiri is a homemade rice ball. Inside, it is filled with Japanese pickles, flakes of seafood or other ingredients. Usually the rice ball is wrapped in seaweed.

Q Do the Japanese use a lot of soy sauce?

Yes, they do. Soy sauce is called *shoyu* in Japanese. It is the main way to flavor food. It is used when cooking food and also to flavor it when you eat. At most tables in Japanese restaurants, you will find a little bottle of soy sauce. You cannot make very many Japanese dishes without using soy sauce.

Q I went to a restaurant and had brown soup with seaweed in it. What was it?

That's *miso shiru* (*miso* soup). *Miso* is made from soybeans, salt and sometimes rice. It is used to make soup, but it is also used to add flavor to other types of Japanese dishes. *Miso* soup is a key food for almost any Japanese meal. A cook in Japan is often judged mainly on his or her *miso* soup.

Q Do Japanese eat a lot of tofu?

Yes. Tofu is very common in Japan. Tofu is now a common ingredient in many parts of the world. There are many ways that you can use it. It is high in protein and low in fat, and it's cheap.

In America, tofu is used to make ice cream and

other food, but I once went to a tofu restaurant in Kyoto and we had a meal with about 10 courses, and everything was made out of tofu. Tofu doesn't have a strong flavor, and so it can be used in a lot of ways. I have a friend in Japan who is an exchange student from America, and she said that she likes to put it in spaghetti sauce and make tofu lasagna. It's a good thing tofu is so good for you.

Q How is seaweed used in Japanese cooking?

There are many types of seaweed. One of the most common types of seaweed is called *wakame*. It is cooked for a short time and used mostly to make soup. Most people put *wakame* in their *miso* soup.

Another type is *konbu*. *Konbu* is not usually eaten alone. It is usually used to flavor food. *Nori* is dried seaweed. A sheet of *nori* is often used to wrap *onigiri* rice balls.

Q Do Japanese eat raw fish every day?

Not every day, but *sashimi* is very popular. Most people like it. *Sashimi* is a little expensive and that's why most Japanese don't eat it every day.

Q Do most Japanese eat a lot of noodles?

Yes, noodles are very popular in Japan. There are noodle shops on almost every corner. *Ramen* (Chinese noodles) is the most popular type, but there are many other types. You might also want to try *soba* (buckwheat noodles) and *udon* (wheat noodles). You can eat noodles hot or cold.

Before coming to Japan, I had eaten a lot of instant noodles. *Ramen* is very cheap in America. Sometimes you can buy packs of noodles for about 10 cents, so it is especially popular with poor students. When I came to Japan, I was very surprised to go to a *ramen* shop and see so many different kinds of *ramen*. They all cost more than 10 cents, but they were certainly better tasting than the *ramen* I ate in college.

❑ Main Dishes

Q What are common Japanese dishes?

Most Japanese are very interested in food. There are many shows about food on TV, and food magazines are also very popular. Here are some traditional Japanese dishes:

Tempura
Tempura is one of the most well-known dishes. It is made by covering vegetables, seafood and other ingredients in batter and then deep-frying them in oil.

Tonkatsu
Tonkatsu is made by covering pork cutlets with a thick batter and frying them in oil. It is served with shredded cabbage and a sauce that is similar to steak sauce.

Sukiyaki

Sukiyaki is a famous dish made with thin slices of beef and vegetables. It is cooked in a pot at the table. All the ingredients are put in the pot together and seasoned with soy sauce and sugar. Most people dip the pieces of cooked beef and vegetable in raw egg and soy sauce before eating them.

Shabu-shabu

Shabu-shabu is another dish cooked at the table. It is also made from very thin slices of beef and vegetables. The ingredients are cooked briefly one at a time in boiling water, which is not as strongly flavored as *sukiyaki*, and then eaten immediately with soy sauce or a sesame or bitter orange dip.

Q Do Japanese usually drink tea when they eat?

Japanese people often drink tea with Japanese food. Japanese tea is green or brown. It is drunk plain, with no sugar, milk, or lemon added.

Tea came to Japan from China in the 12th century as a type of medicine. When you go to a Japanese-style restaurant, it is usually served free.

But many Japanese drink alcohol with dinner. *Sake*, *shochu*, and wine are very popular, but beer is probably the most popular.

Q What do Japanese eat for dessert?

Western-style cakes and desserts are very popular in Japan today, but baking ovens are not a part of the typical Japanese kitchen. Traditional Japanese desserts are usually made from rice and beans. The rice is often pounded to make a dough. It is then placed around the bean paste. There are many types of tasty traditional desserts, but the dessert isn't only for eating. It is also pretty to look at.

Q What is Japanese tableware like?

In the West, dishes usually come in a complete

set, all of the same color and style. But a traditional Japanese meal is served on small dishes and plates of many different colors and styles. There is no requirement that they match.

Some dishes made by master craftsman are very expensive, but you can also go to special markets where less expensive dishes are sold. Instead of trying to buy one entire set of the same style, you might want to get a lot of different styles.

Q What kind of food is popular when people eat out?

According to a survey in 2000 by the Institute for Free Time Design, the most popular leisure activity was dining out. Although there are many different types of restaurants in Japan, the restaurants that serve traditional Japanese food are the most popular. Most specialize in one type of food, such as, *sukiyaki*, *tempura* or *tonkatsu*. But *kaitenzushi* and *ramen* shops are probably the most popular.

It is unusual for Japanese to invite friends and colleagues home for a meal in Japan, so restaurants or coffee shops are the main meeting places for socializing and celebrating special occasions. For large groups, many restaurants offer a set meal for a low price, often with an all-you-can-drink option.

In large cities, restaurants specializing in foreign foods are becoming popular—especially those serving Italian, Chinese and Korean dishes. And fast-food restaurants like McDonalds are everywhere!

I remember one evening, a long time ago, when I went to a Japanese pub with some friends. I didn't want to drink any alcohol and neither did the other foreigners I went with. We just ordered food and didn't order any drinks. But the restaurant charged us about ¥5,000 for drinks. I was very upset and I argued with the manager. I even wanted to call the police. But my friends said that we should just pay and go. Most restaurants in Japan are honest and friendly, but you still need to be careful, especially at night.

4. Traveling in Japan

❑ Trains

Q: What's the best way to travel around Japan?

If you want to go from one city to another, airplanes are popular, but the Shinkansen "bullet trains" are faster, easier, and go to more places. Shinkansen trains leave Tokyo Station about every 15 minutes, so they are very convenient. But if you have a lot of heavy baggage, it might be difficult to go up and down all the station stairs.

Q: Are the trains in Tokyo and other big cities very crowded?

In the mornings and evenings, the trains are very crowded. Unless you have to, try to avoid using the trains from 7:00 to 9:00 a.m. and from 6:00 to 8:00 p.m. During these hours, it is very difficult to get on and off trains because they are filled with people.

But you don't have to run to catch a train in Tokyo. Trains run every few minutes, so you can catch the next one. On the Yamanote Line, trains run every three minutes. But they are all crowded during rush hour.

I once had a really busy day scheduled. I needed to get from one appointment to another and had just enough time to get there on the train if I ran. I told my friend about this, and he volunteered to take me by car. He said that I could get there twice as fast by car. It was a really important appointment, and so I appreciated his kindness. In the end, it took me twice as long to get there by car, and I missed the important appointment. I was kind of mad at my friend. Trains in Japan can be really crowded, but at least they run on time.

Q How fast are Shinkansen trains?

They can go as fast as 350 kilometers per hour, but they usually go much slower. To go from Tokyo to Osaka (about 553 kilometers), it takes a little over two hours. The same journey using local trains would take 9 to 10 hours. Airplanes are faster, but it takes a long time to check in and out at the airport.

When the Shinkansen first ran in 1964, it was the fastest train in the world. The French TGV train now holds the speed record for normal passenger trains, at 515 kph.

Q What other special features do the Shinkansen have?

The Green Car coaches are like first-class air travel. The seats are larger and more luxurious, and free drinks and newspapers are brought to the seats.*

In the normal carriages, the smoking coaches are filled with smoke, so non-smokers should be sure to reserve non-smoking seats. The feature which always surprises foreigners is that the seats can be turned around, so you can have private seats facing the front, or turn the seat around to face backwards and face the people behind. This is especially useful if you are traveling with friends.

---

* Payment required for some train lines.

Part 3 Japanese Life and Culture

Q How about eating on trains?

When Japanese travel by train, they like to eat *ekiben*. These are special boxed lunches. They don't cost very much and most of them taste very good. You can buy them on the platforms of the train stations. But *ekiben* should only be eaten on long-distance trains. No one eats *bento*, or much of anything else, on local or subway trains.

❑ Driving in Japan

Q Is driving in Japan difficult?

Japan has one of the best rail systems in the world, but there are many times when the train can't take you where you want to go. When this happens, most people travel by car.

The first thing you'll notice is that the Japanese drive on the left side of the road. For people who come from Australia and the U.K., this is not a problem, but for everybody else, this can take time to get used to. Driving in Japan is generally very safe and most drivers are careful and friendly, but you have to look out for people walking and riding bicycles, especially when turning left. You must get a special certificate from the police to show you have a parking place before you can buy a car.

Q Is it expensive to drive in Japan?

Driving in Japan can be quite expensive for a number of reasons. It may cost a lot just to park your car. The price of gasoline is higher than in the U.S., but it is about the same as in Europe. Toll expressways in Japan can be expensive, unless there is a group of you who can share the cost. But the advantage is that the expressways are more direct and less congested than regular roads.

❑ Tourism

Q Do Japanese travel abroad a lot?

Because Japanese people work so hard, most people

vacation at the same time: at the New Year, in Golden Week (April/May) and during *O-bon* (August). You'll find that prices are most expensive at these times. According to a 2000 survey by the Institute for Free Time Design, Japanese spent more money on overseas travel than any other leisure activity. Most people go overseas for sightseeing and 15% for business. Popular destinations are Hawaii, Hong Kong, Saipan, Guam, Australia, and Europe.

Recently, travel agents have recognized that Japanese mothers and grandparents often travel overseas with their daughters or granddaughters, so companies are starting to target these groups, offering tours that include art, culture and shopping.

Q Do Japanese travel a lot in Japan?

Domestic travel is the third most popular leisure activity in Japan after eating out and driving. Many people take short, weekend holidays, often to ski resorts or *onsen* hot springs. Many Japanese enjoy sporting activities, such as golf, hiking, skiing and diving.

Japan FAQ

❑ Famous Places/Sightseeing

Q What are the most famous places to visit?

There are many interesting places to go in Japan. It is said that the three most beautiful places are Amanohashidate (Kyoto Pref.), Miyajima (Hiroshima Pref.) and Matsushima (Miyagi Pref.), but the most popular destinations for Japanese are Mt. Fuji, Kyoto, Kyushu, and Okinawa.

Popular daytrips from Tokyo include: Kamakura's Giant Buddha, temples and shrines; Ashinoko lake and Yumoto hot springs in Hakone; Toshogu Shrine, the Three Monkeys and the Kegon Falls at Nikko. For the young and the young at heart, you might want to visit Tokyo Disneyland. And during the summer, many people like to climb Mt. Fuji.

Q What is it like to climb Mt. Fuji?

Mt. Fuji is the tallest mountain in Japan. It is 3,776 meters high. The best time to climb Mt. Fuji is from July 1 to August 31. In other seasons, there is too much snow at the top.

There are three different trails to the top of Mt. Fuji: the Fujinomiya Trail, the Gotenba Trail, and the Subashiri Trail. The Fujinomiya Trail, on the south side, is the easiest route. From here you can see Suruga Bay and Izu Peninsula as you climb. You can go to the 2,400-meter level by car. At the 5th station (Gogome), there is a resting place and advice center. At the 8th station (Hachigo-me) you can stop at a clinic if you are injured or don't feel well. Most people take between five and seven hours to climb from the Gogome level to the top. But coming down only takes two or three hours.

Japan FAQ

Q How about World Heritage Sites in Japan?

World Heritage Sites are quite popular in Japan as tourist destinations.

The most famous ones are Kyoto, Nara, Nikko, and the Hiroshima Peace Memorial.

Sacred Sites and Pilgrimage Routes in the Kii Mountain Range are recently registered World Heritage Sites and have already become popular destinations for Japanese tourists.

Q What are Japanese-style hotels like?

There are Japanese inns or *ryokan* everywhere—in cities and country areas. Some inns are very new, but others are hundreds of years old. In a Japanese inn, you can sleep on tatami mats and enjoy Japanese food, flowers and music. Some inns are very beautiful and set in beautiful surroundings.

When you arrive, you must take your shoes off at the entrance. The hostess of the inn will take you to your room so you can relax while drinking green tea. Dinner will probably be served in your room. Some inns are very simple, but some serve very expensive meals with many different dishes. The menu is usually set, so you don't need to order.

There are also modern hotels almost everywhere you go in Japan. These hotels are almost the same as hotels in Europe and the United States.

❏ *Onsen* and *Sento*

Q What is an *onsen*?

An *onsen* is a natural, mineral spa bath. The temperature of the water is usually higher than 25°C (77°F). Japan has a lot of volcanoes, and so this means that hot springs can be found almost anywhere. Many contain special minerals from the rocks. This is thought to help improve the health and even to help sick people get better. Japanese people often enjoy spas, especially *rotenburo,* or open-air baths, in beautiful surroundings.

Q What are public baths like?

For a long time, the only way most people could take a bath was to go to a *sento* or public bath. There were *sento* all over Japan. Although there are fewer *sento* now, there are still about 5,500 *sento* in Japan and 1,000 in Tokyo. Today, most Japanese have baths in their home, but still go to a *sento* sometimes because it feels good.

5 Japanese Leisure

❏ Free Time

Q What do people do in their free time?

The number one activity is eating out! But other popular activities include *karaoke*, watching videos, going to the movies, concerts, and sports events, or playing pachinko.

Domestic travel is also very popular. Many people travel to the mountains in winter to go skiing and snowboarding. In summer they go to the seaside. And everyone likes going to hot springs resorts in every season!

Q Do Japanese like sports?

Exercising is a very popular activity in Japan. Many people belong to a sports club, where they go regularly to swim, run, use the gym, or join an exercise class.

Golf, fishing, jogging, baseball, and skiing are particularly popular. Traditional martial arts, like judo, karate and kendo, are also popular, but it takes many years of practice to get good at them.

Q What kind of sports do Japanese like to watch?

The Japanese like to watch professional sports such as baseball, soccer, and sumo. Everyone supports Japanese players who have become internationally successful. In the last few years, several Japanese baseball players have done well in Major League Baseball in the United States, and some Japanese soccer players have succeeded on European teams. These athletes are a source of national pride for Japan.

Every four years, Japan is hit by Olympic fever. Japanese athletes who win gold medals at the Olympic Games become celebrities and often make a lot of money appearing in commercials.

Q Where are good things to do on weekends?

There are many things you can do! If you want to relax, you could go to a hot spring resort. There are many *onsen* in Japan, but places like Hakone, are particularly popular. Many *onsen* are believed to cure illneses.

If you want to experience some history and culture, you should visit Nikko. Nikko has a shrine for Tokugawa Ieyasu, the first shogun of the Edo Period. There are also beautiful waterfalls and you can see the famous carvings of the three monkeys that mean "Hear no evil, see no evil, speak no evil." Nikko is also a good place to get close to nature and go hiking.

For something more modern, you could visit Tokyo Disneyland. No matter when you go, it will probably be crowded, but you can still have a good time.

❑ Shopping

Q Where are the most fashionable places to go shopping?

The most fashionable places in Tokyo are Ginza, Shibuya, Harajuku and Shinjuku.

Ginza means "silver seat." This is where you can find many expensive and high-fashion department stores, so it's especially popular with wealthy housewives.

Shibuya and Harajuku are popular with teenagers, because they have a lot of fashionable shops and stalls selling clothes and accessories. On Sundays, dozens of young people dress up in Goth style and other costumes and meet near Harajuku Station.

Shinjuku is famous for its skyscrapers and has many department stores, including international shops.

Q Where can you buy the latest electronic products?

The best place is Akihabara, two stops north of Tokyo Station. Here you can buy the very latest

Japanese electronic products and gadgets. If you buy electronic products to use overseas, remember to ask if they can be used in your country. Japanese products mostly run on 100 volts.

Q What are good souvenirs from Japan?

Black Japanese lacquerware is world-famous. Genuine lacquerware is expensive and delicate, but imitation goods are less expensive and popular, especially small lunch boxes, which can be used as jewelry boxes.

Ukiyo-e prints, Japanese pottery and ceramics are also famous, but expensive. Small *sake* cups are also popular and they don't cost so much. Goods made from Japanese paper or antique kimono, such as bags, purses, and so on, make nice and not so expensive gifts.

Q What are the department stores like?

Japanese department stores are very large. But most of the large chain stores are similar inside. The basement floor sells Japanese sweets, cakes, coffee, wine, etc. and is often connected to a subway station.

The 1st floor, at ground level, sells a variety of seasonal goods: cosmetics, jewelry and clothing accessories. The 2nd and 3rd floors have designer clothes for women and men. Other floors sell toys, stationery, electronic goods, CDs, household items, wedding clothes and so on. Every floor has a lot of brand-name goods.

6. Japanese Tradition

❑ Japanese Festivals

Q What are the most famous festivals in Japan?

There are festivals every month somewhere in Japan. The most famous festivals in Tokyo are the Sanno Matsuri, the Sanja Matsuri and the Kanda Matsuri.

These date back to the Edo Period and are always crowded with people following the *mikoshi* (portable shrines) as they are carried around the area. Other popular festivals are: the Sapporo Yuki Matsuri with giant snow sculptures; the Gion Matsuri in Kyoto in July, with beautiful tall floats; and the Sendai Tanabata Star Matsuri.

Hanami, or cherry-blossom viewing, is a national event, when everyone sits under the cherry trees, eating, drinking, and singing songs. *Hanabi* firework displays in summer are also popular.

Q What's the biggest holiday in Japan?

In most Western countries, the biggest holiday is Christmas, but in Japan it is the New Year. There are a lot of things to do to prepare for January 1. This is the time to clean the home and office. People place a *kadomatsu* pine-tree decoration outside their homes and make special food called *osechi-ryori*, a variety of dishes which can be preserved for eating over the several days of holiday.

It is also traditionally a time to visit friends and business acquaintances, but nowadays most people just send *nengajo* greeting cards.

Q: Where do people go for the New Year holiday?

Many people live in big cities. During the holidays, they often go back to their parents' home in the country. If you work for a company in Japan, it is sometimes difficult to take time off. But the New Year is a very special occasion when everyone can take holidays.

Most Japanese start the new year by going to a nearby *jinja* shrine or *otera* temple. They pray for health and happiness in the coming year. This is called *hatsumode*. The most famous temples for *hatsumode* in Japan are Meiji Jingu Shrine in Tokyo and Tsurugaoka Hachimangu Shrine in Kamakura. Over a million people go to these shrines for *hatsumode* in the first three days of the New Year. If you go, you may have to wait in line for a long time before you can very briefly pray in front of the altar.

Q: What do Japanese do on Christmas Day?

Christmas is not a holiday in Japan, but there are many Christmas things and events all over Japan.

People put up decorations, give each other gifts, and eat Christmas cake. There are not very many Christians in Japan, but Christmas does feel like a big holiday. On December 26, all the Christmas decorations are quickly replaced with New Year decorations.

Q What are the other holidays in Japan?

There are 15 national holidays each year. They are all celebrated slightly differently in each area of Japan, but all schools, government offices, and most businesses close on these days. When the holiday falls on a Sunday, it is observed on the following Monday.

Here are some of them:
- *Ganjitsu*, January 1, celebrated as New Year's Day.
- The second Monday in January is Coming-of-Age Day (*Seijin-no-hi*). This is the day when 20-year-olds born between April 2 of the previous year and April 1 of that year celebrate becoming adults.
- Vernal Equinox Day (*Shunbun-no-hi*) is around March 21. Autumnal Equinox Day (*Shubun-no-hi*) is around September 23. It is during the week

of *Higan*, a Buddhist holiday. In this week, families pray for family members who have died. They sweep, clean and purify the area around the grave, and offer up flowers and food.
- Children's Day (*Kodomo-no-hi*) is on May 5. This is a day when everyone prays for the health and happiness of children. It was originally called *Tango-no-Sekku*, or the Boys' Festival. On this day, families with boys display warrior dolls inside their home and fly *koi-nobori* (carp streamers) outside. They eat *chimaki* (rice dumplings) and *kashiwamochi* (sweet-bean-paste-filled rice cakes).

Q What other traditional events are there?

There are many traditional events that take place throughout Japan every year. Although they vary from place to place, many are associated with rice harvests (sowing or harvesting), the lunar calendar or the seasons.

Setsubun, February 3 or 4
Setsubun is for celebrating the end of winter and

the first day of spring, *Risshun*. It falls on February 3 or 4. In almost all homes, a *mame-maki* ceremony takes place. People throw beans while shouting "Oni wa soto, fuku wa uchi!" (Devils out, good luck in!) either in their homes, or in a public place like a temple.

Hina-matsuri, March 3

In homes with little girls, *hina-ningyo* dolls are displayed, usually including an emperor and empress dressed in Heian court style. Dolls are often passed down from generation to generation, so the displays can sometimes be hundreds of years old. Multicolored rice cakes and *sake* are also displayed.

Hanami—Cherry-blossom viewing

There are *sakura* (cherry) trees all over Japan. Since a long time ago, people have gathered under the cherry blossoms in early April to eat, drink, sing, and enjoy the beautiful *sakura* trees.

Tanabata, July 7

The *tanabata* star festival is celebrated on July 7. *Tanabata* is one of the most popular *matsuri* festivals in Japan. It commemorates the meeting of two star lovers, Altair and Vega, who can only meet in the

Milky Way once a year on this day. People write their wishes on colored strips of paper and tie them to branches of bamboo trees. They hope their dreams will come true.

O-bon, August 13 to 16

O-bon is the biggest Buddhist holiday in Japan, second only to the Shinto New Year's celebrations. From August 13 to 16, businesses close and people go to their parents' homes in the country. On the 13th, people light fires and display fruit and vegetables near the entrances of their homes, to guide the spirits of their ancestors back.

During this time, people gather in public places to perform *O-bon* dances, to send the spirits of the ancestors away at the end of *O-bon*.

Tsukimi—Moon viewing

Tsukimi is the time to appreciate the full moon. The moon on August 15 of the lunar calendar is called *jugoya* and the moon of September 13 of the lunar calendar is called *ato-no-tsukimi*. *Tsukimi* is usually celebrated on *jugoya* by eating *dango* (a Japanese sweet) under the full moon.

Shichi-go-san, November 15

The 7-5-3 Festival, is the time to celebrate the growth of a child. It is a special day for 5-year-old boys and 3-year-old or 7-year-old girls. On November 15, children are dressed in their best clothes. Girls usually wear expensive kimonos and boys wear *haori* and *hakama* (kimono with a loose jacket and pleated trousers). Their parents take them to a *jinja* shrine to pray for their health and growth.

Q Is it true the Japanese see a rabbit when they look at the moon?

Yes. In many Western countries, people say that they can see the face of a man in the moon. But in Japan and China, people say they can see a rabbit making *mochi* rice cakes on the moon.

❏ Japanese Traditional Arts

Q What is kabuki?

Kabuki theater started about 400 years ago. It was

started by a woman named Izumo-no-Okuni at the end of the 16th century. Many people are surprised by this because today all the actors are male. Most of the women who acted in kabuki at the time were prostitutes, and so the Tokugawa government made it illegal for women to take part in kabuki performances. The male actors who play the female parts are called *onnagata*.

Kabuki is popular because the scenery and costumes are beautiful. Together with the expert acting, kabuki re-creates beautiful scenes and stories from Japanese history.

Some plays are serious, even tragic, and others are comedies.

Q What other forms of Japanese theater are there?

Noh is another Japanese form of theater. It started about 600 years ago. The movement of the actors and the masks are beautiful, but it is very difficult to understand, even for native Japanese! The largest *noh* theater is in Tokyo where there are shows almost every day, but smaller performances are also given around

Japan, usually at Shinto shrines. *Bunraku* theater, using large dolls operated by three men, is also very popular.

Q Is it expensive to see Japanese theater?

Kabuki, *bunraku* and *noh* are expensive, especially if you buy tickets for good seats for a whole program. But sometimes you can buy cheaper tickets to see one kabuki act from the upper gallery.

You can also see traditional Japanese performances at many festivals. There is a festival going on somewhere in Japan almost every day of the year. You can see performances of Japanese music, drama, magic, and much more.

Q When did the tea ceremony start?

The tea ceremony, *chanoyu*, originated in China and came to Japan in the Muromachi Period. It is considered an art form, incorporating Zen customs, art and simple beauty. It was refined by Sen-no-Rikyu in the 16th century and has since developed into a number of schools, which are still popular today. The three most popular ones are Omote Senke, Ura Senke and Mushanokoji Senke (all started by descendents of Sen-no-Rikyu).

Q What is *ikebana*?

Ikebana is Japanese flower arrangement. It was originally performed by Buddhist monks in the 6th century to decorate the temple altar. Classic *ikebana* designs are based on an asymmetrical triangle.

Today there are over 3,000 schools with over 20 million students. The most famous schools are Ohara, Ikenobo and Sogetsu. Many foreigners enjoy learning *ikebana*. But because it is a very expensive hobby and takes many, many years to learn, few foreigners continue to study and become *ikebana* teachers.

The important thing with *ikebana* isn't just the finished product. The mind of the person doing the *ikebana* and an understanding of nature are also important.

❑ Sports and Martial Arts

Q Which is more popular in Japan, baseball or soccer?

Baseball is probably still more popular than soccer, but soccer is becoming more popular every year. The J-League is the professional soccer league in Japan. It started in 1993. In 1999, it became two divisions, J1 and J2. In 1998, the Japan National Soccer Team went to France to participate in the World Cup for the first time. Then in 2002, the World Cup took place in Japan and Korea.

Part 3 Japanese Life and Culture

Q When did the Japanese start playing baseball?

Baseball came to Japan in 1873, just five years after the end of the Tokugawa shogunate. Some Japanese students played a series of games with Americans living in Yokohama and sailors from naval ships. After the first game, the Japanese team came back and won several games. This helped to make baseball very popular in Japan.

Q Is sumo a very old sport?

Yes, it is. It is not known when it first started, but it is thought to be about 2,000 years old. But it did not become a real sport until the 17th century.

The aim of the sport is to force the other wrestler out of the *dohyo* ring or make him touch it with any part of his body apart from his feet. The success of some wrestlers from foreign countries has helped to increase the popularity of sumo in Japan and also in other countries around the world.

Here are the tournament months and the sites: January–Tokyo, March–Osaka, May–Tokyo, July–

Nagoya, September–Tokyo, and November–Fukuoka.

Q What about the Japanese martial arts?

Martial arts are very popular in Japan, but most of the tournaments are not shown on television. Judo was created by a man named Jigoro Kano (1860–1938). It combines strength with softness. Karate is a martial art that combines punching, kicking and blocking. It came from China to Okinawa, in southern Japan, in the 16th century. The word kendo means "the way of the sword." It is the oldest of all the Japanese martial arts. The swords used are made of bamboo and weigh about 500 grams.

7 Japanese Custom

❏ The Japanese Way of Thinking

Q What are Japan's main religions?

The main religions in Japan are Shinto, Buddhism and Christianity.

Only 30% of Japanese believe in one religion; most believe in several. For example, births and weddings are celebrated at Shinto shrines, and funerals are held at Buddhist temples. Most people also celebrate Christmas. One explanation for this religious freedom could be that until 1868 Buddhism and Shinto were considered one religion.

Q What does "Japan is a vertical society" mean?

A "vertical society" means that you have respect for

others above you, in school, at work, and also within the family. The language people use in Japan changes according to the rank of the person they are talking to and whether they are senior or junior to them.

Q Is it true the Japanese don't express their opinions very clearly?

Yes. One reason is because the language is very indirect. Japanese tend to avoid saying such words as "I," "you," or "no," and so they must find other indirect ways to say the same thing. Another reason is that Japanese worry a lot about what other people think, and they avoid saying what they really think. They like to try to maintain group harmony.

Q How do Japanese maintain group harmony?

Group harmony is very important for Japanese people. It is important for everyone to get along, even if this means ignoring some facts or openly speaking the truth. This is known as *honne-to-tatemae* in Japanese.

Let's say that your boss is so mean and every night at home you curse him. This is *honne* (the truth). But at the office, you never say something against him and sometimes even praise him. This is *tatemae* (saving face). In Japan, *tatemae* is very important for maintaining harmony, especially in the workplace.

❑ Japanese Things

Q Why do the Japanese give a lot of gifts?

The two times when gifts are given the most is at the end of the year and in summer. The gifts given at the end of the year are called *oseibo*. The gifts given in the summer are called *ochugen*.

In Japan, gifts are part of greetings, and when you receive a gift from someone, you should send something back. Sometimes, the same person will then send you another gift and it goes on. Lately, young people don't think very much about this custom and fewer gifts are exchanged among the younger generations.

Japan FAQ

Q Why do many restaurants have a curtain at the entrance?

This curtain is called a *noren*. When there is a *noren* at the front of a shop, customers know that it is open. There are many types of *noren,* and they make good souvenirs to take home with you.

Q What is *bonsai*?

Bonsai is the art of growing miniature trees. The grower controls how the tree grows by cutting the roots, tying the branches and controlling the amount of water and sunlight the tree gets.

A *bonsai* tree does not have to be realistic, but it should reflect the taste of the artist. It can take 100 years to grow a good *bonsai*, so the trees are usually passed down in a family from one generation to the next.

Q What is the large piece of cloth people carry things in?

This is called a *furoshiki*. It is simply a square piece

of cloth. You put whatever you want to carry inside of it and then tie the corners together. It's kind of like a Japanese suitcase. Although most people now use Western suitcases and bags, some people still use the *furoshiki* as a convenient way to carry things.

Q When do ghosts appear in Japan?

In most Western countries, ghosts seem to come out in the fall near the time of Halloween. But in Japan, the summer is the time for ghosts. This is around the Buddhist holiday known as *O-bon,* when the Japanese spirits of dead ancestors come back to earth. In the summer, the weather is hot and humid. This seems to make the right atmosphere for ghosts in Japan.

Q What are the big red paper lanterns in front of shops?

They are made of paper pasted over bamboo and put in front of bars that serve *sake* and some simple dishes. It means that the shop is now open. When you see an *aka-chochin*, you also know that the prices are not too expensive. Such bars are similar to English pubs.

Q What are the little red stamps on Japanese documents?

These are *hanko* seals. Most *hanko* are a little thicker than a pencil and are about five centimeters long. They have the owner's name carved into the end so they can use it as a stamp. Japanese usually use their *hanko* instead of signing their names.

Some *hanko* are made from wood or plastic and don't cost very much, but some of them are very expensive. People usually have one special *hanko* that is registered at the city office. This *hanko* is for official purposes, and so if someone steals it, they might be able to take money out of your bank account or sell your property.

Most *hanko* that Japanese have are in *kanji*. But when foreigners live in Japan, they often make a *hanko* with their name written in *katakana* instead of *kanji*.

PART 3 JAPANESE LIFE AND CULTURE

❑ Modern Japan

Q What does *anime* mean?

In Japanese, *anime* means "animation." *Anime* television shows are very popular. In America and other countries, animation is mostly for children, but in Japan it is for everyone. There are *anime* about almost every topic you can think of. You can see a lot of *anime* movies and *anime* shows on TV.

Q When did modern *anime* start?

The kind of *anime* that we see today started in the 1960s. The first popular *anime* was called "Tetsuwan Atom." It was shown on television in Japan from 1963 to 1966. Tetsuwan Atom came from a comic series that started in 1952, created by Osamu Tezuka.

In the 1950s, Tezuka was the most popular comic-strip artist in Japan. He wanted to try and make *anime* himself. Most *anime* at that time were about old stories, but he decided to make a modern *anime* based on Tetsuwan Atom. This *anime* became very popular in Japan. Some people call Osamu the "Walt Disney of Japan."

In 1963, "Tetsuwan Atom" was shown on television in the U.S. But it was re-named *Astro Boy*. It soon became a big hit in many parts of the world.

Q Who are the famous *anime* artists now?

Probably the most famous are Hayao Miyazaki and Isao Takahata. In the 1980s, Miyazaki worked for a large publishing company. He made a magazine for people who liked to read about *anime*. With his friend, Isao Takahata, he made many *anime* films that became very famous in Japan, such as *My Neighbor Totoro* (1988), *Kiki's Delivery Service* (1989), *The Crimson Pig* (1992), *Grave of the Fireflies* (1988), and *Pom Poko* (1994). *Pom Poko* was nominated for the Academy Awards Best Foreign Film Oscar.

In the last few years, many *anime* by Miyazaki have been very popular in Japan and also in other countries, especially *My Neighbor Totoro* and *Princess Mononoke*. But the most internationally famous Japanese *anime* is called *Spirited Away*. (*Sen to Chihiro no Kami-kakushi* in Japanese.) This *anime* received the Oscar for Best Animated Feature Film at the 75th Annual Academy Awards. It made more money than any other Japanese film in history. In Japan, more people saw *Spirited Away* than *Titanic*.

Q How do young children spend their time?

In days past, children met in parks and vacant lots to play catch or other games. But now the most popular pastime for young children is probably home-video games. It is also a cause of worry for parents. Parents often say they have to pull their children away from these games so they will do their homework. But most parents have given up. They realize that if their children don't know anything about home-video games, they might not be able to make friends at school.

Q Do Japanese like ghost movies?

Yes, ghost and horror movies have been very

popular in Japan in recent years. Some of these movies such as *The Ring* and *The Grudge* (*Juon* in Japanese) have been remade by Hollywood. It is difficult to make a big action movie in Japan, but it is possible to make very scary ghost and horror movies on a small budget. But before ghost movies, there were ghost stories. In fact, Japanese ghost movies have roots going back to classical Japanese literature and theater.

Q What are the little things hanging from mobile phones?

For many people, especially young people, the mobile phone is more than just a tool for talking to people. When they buy one, they often change the color or give it a unique design. They also tie on little decorations. Most people change the ringing sound for calls from different people. And some people even make their own tune. It is a way to tell people who you are and express your identity.

Q: Why are the Japanese so interested in blood types?

Many people in Japan think that you can tell a lot about a person by their blood type. There are many shows on TV that talk about this. Japanese believe that different blood types have different personalities and talents.

Type A people want to avoid fighting and they get along well with other people. They are also motivated and want to do well in everything they try. This is a common type in Japan.

Type B people are honest and like to do things their own way. They have a lot of energy and like to be organized.

Type O people are loyal and have many good friends. They like to look good and often get embarrassed.

Type AB people like to make others feel happy. It's sometimes hard for them to make difficult decisions.

Q: Is that real food in the restaurant window?

No, it's actually made from wax. The restaurants

order models of the dishes they serve. If you go to Kappabashi in Tokyo, you can see the shops where craftsman make these wax pieces of art called "samples." You can even buy key chains with wax food hanging from them. They make great souvenirs. In Kappabashi, you'll also see dozens of other shops selling things used to cook and serve food.

Q Are shops open at night?

If there is one thing that is common in Japan, it's convenience stores. When I first came to Japan in the early 1980s, there weren't so many convenience stores at all. I asked a Japanese friend about this, and he said that convenience stores didn't fit in well with the Japanese lifestyle.

Now you can often find 10 or more convenience stores within walking distance. The result has been heated competition. Convenience stores compete with each other to provide the best products and the most convenient services.

Q Are there any discount stores?

Yes. It costs a lot of money to live in Japan, but there are things you can do to save money. One of the easiest is to find a "¥100 shop." These shops have almost everything you need to set up house in Japan. Some bigger shops even have clothes and food. They are sometimes called the "housewives' paradise." Happy shopping!

Word List

- 本文で使われている全ての語を掲載しています (LEVEL 1、2)。ただし、LEVEL 3以上は、中学校レベルの語を含みません。
- 語形が規則変化する語の見出しは原形で示しています。不規則変化語は本文中で使われている形になっています。
- 一般的な意味を紹介していますので、一部の語で本文で実際に使われている品詞や意味と合っていないことがあります。
- 品詞は以下のように示しています。

名 名詞	代 代名詞	形 形容詞	副 副詞	動 動詞	助 助動詞
前 前置詞	接 接続詞	間 間投詞	冠 冠詞	略 略語	俗 俗語
熟 熟語	頭 接頭語	尾 接尾語	記 記号	関 関係代名詞	

A

- □ **abolish** 動 廃止する, 撤廃する
- □ **Academy Award** 名 アカデミー賞《アメリカの映画賞》
- □ **accept** 動 ①〜を受け入れる ②〜に同意する, 〜を認める
- □ **accessory** 名 付属品, 装飾品, アクセサリー
- □ **accordance** 名 一致, 適合 in accordance with〜 〜に従って
- □ **according** 副《-to》〜によれば[よると]
- □ **account** 名 ①計算書 ②勘定, 預金口座 ③報告 動 〜を…とみなす
- □ **accountant** 名 税理士, 会計士
- □ **accurate** 形 ①正確な, 間違いのない ②精密な
- □ **achievement** 名 ①達成, 成就 ②業績
- □ **acquaintance** 名 ①知人, 知り合い ②面識, 知識
- □ **act** 名 行為, 行ない 動 ①行動する ②機能する ③〜を演じる
- □ **active** 形 ①活動的な ②積極的な ③活動[作動]中の
- □ **activity** 名 活動, 活気
- □ **actor** 名 俳優, 役者
- □ **actually** 副 実際に, 本当に
- □ **AD** 略 西暦(紀元)
- □ **add** 動 〜を(…に)加える, 足す
- □ **adjective** 名 形容詞 形 形容詞的な
- □ **admit** 動 認める, 許す
- □ **adopt** 動 ①採択する, 選ぶ ②承認する ③〜を養子にする
- □ **adult** 名 大人, 成人 形 大人の, 成人した
- □ **advanced** 形 ①前にある, 進んだ ②進歩した, 高等の
- □ **advantage** 名 有利な点[立場], 強み, 優越
- □ **adverb** 名 副詞 形 副詞の
- □ **advice center** 名 案内所
- □ **affair** 名 事柄, 事件, 問題
- □ **affect** 動 ①〜に影響する ②(病気などが)〜を冒す 名 感情, 欲望
- □ **agent** 名 ①代理人 ②代表者
- □ **aging** 形 年老いた, 老朽化した, 高年齢化した 名 老化, 年老いること
- □ **agreement** 名 ①合意, 協定 ②一致
- □ **aid** 名 援助(者), 助け 動 〜を援助

WORD LIST

する, ~を助ける, ~を手伝う
- **aim** 動①(武器・カメラなど)を向ける ②~をねらう, ~を目指す 名ねらい, 目標
- **airplane** 名飛行機
- **Alaska** 名アラスカ《地名》
- **alcohol** 名アルコール(飲料)
- **alcove** 名アルコーブ《部屋の一部引っ込んだところ》, 床の間
- **alike** 形よく似ている 副同様に
- **all-you-can-drink** 名飲み放題
- **allied forces** 名多国籍軍, 連合軍, 同盟軍
- **ally** 名同盟国[者] 動~と手を組む
- **alphabet** 名①アルファベット ②~の初歩
- **Altair** 名アルタイル, 彦星, 牽牛星
- **altar** 名祭壇
- **although** 接~だけれども, ~にもかかわらず, たとえ~でも
- **amendment** 名①改正, 修正 ②(憲法の)改正案
- **America** 名アメリカ
- **American** 形アメリカ[人・式]の
- **amount** 名①量, 額 ②《the-》(~の)合計 動(総計)~になる
- **ancestor** 名先祖, 祖先
- **ancient** 形昔の, 古代の
- **Anglo-Japanese Alliance** 名日英同盟
- **animated** 形①活気に満ちた, 生きているような ②アニメの animated cartoon アニメーション, 動画
- **animation** 名①活気, 生気 ②アニメーション, アニメ製作
- **annual** 形年1回の, 例年の, 年次の annual leave 年次(有給)休暇 名①年報 ②一年生植物
- **anthem** 名賛歌, 祝歌 national anthem 国歌
- **antique** 形①古風な, 年代物の ②

ギリシャ・ローマ時代の 名骨董品
- **anymore** 副《通例否定文, 疑問文で》今はもう, これ以上, これから
- **anyone** 代①《疑問文, 条件節で》誰か ②《否定文で》誰も(~ない) ③《肯定文で》誰でも
- **anywhere** 副どこかへ[に], どこにも[へも], どこにでも
- **apart from** 熟~は別として
- **apartment** 名アパート
- **appear** 動①現れる, 見えてくる ②(~のように)見える, ~らしい
- **appointment** 名①(会合などの)約束, 予約 ②任命, 指名
- **appreciate** 動①~を正しく評価する, ~の良さがわかる ②ありがたく思う
- **approval** 名①賛成 ②承認, 認可
- **approve** 動賛成する, 承認する
- **approximately** 副おおよそ, だいたい
- **argue** 動①~を論じる, 議論する ②~と主張する
- **arrange** 動①~を並べる, ~を整える ②~をとり決める ③手配する
- **arrangement** 名①準備, 手配 ②取り決め, 協定 ③整頓 flower arrangement 華道, 生け花
- **arrest** 動逮捕する 名逮捕
- **article** 名①(法令・誓約などの)箇条, 項目 ②(新聞・雑誌などの)記事
- **artisan** 名職人, 熟練工
- **artist** 名芸術家
- **as of now** 熟今(現在)のところ
- **ash** 名灰
- **Asia** 名アジア
- **Asian** 名アジア人 形アジアの
- **assassinate** 動①暗殺する ②(名誉や人格を)傷つける
- **assistant** 名助手, 補佐, 店員 形援助の, 補佐の

- □ **associate** 動①連合［共同］する，提携する ②～と結び付ける ③交際する 名仲間，組合員 形連合した
- □ **Astro Boy** 名鉄腕アトム
- □ **asymmetrical** 形非対称の
- □ **athlete** 名運動選手
- □ **Atlantic Ocean** 名大西洋
- □ **atmosphere** 名①大気 ②雰囲気，周囲の状況
- □ **attack** 動①～を襲う，攻める ②～を非難する ③(病気が)～を冒す 名①攻撃，非難 ②発作，発病
- □ **attend** 動①出席する，参列する ②対応する
- □ **Australia** 名オーストラリア《国名》
- □ **author** 名著者，作家 動～を著する，～を創作する
- □ **Autumnal Equinox Day** 名秋分の日
- □ **average** 名平均，並み 形平均の，普通の 動平均して～になる
- □ **avoid** 動～を避ける，～をしないようにする

B

- □ **background** 名①背景 ②前歴，生い立ち
- □ **backwards** 形①後方(の)へ ②遅れた 副後方へ
- □ **baggage** 名手荷物
- □ **bake** 動オーブンで焼く
- □ **ballot** 名①投票用紙 ②投票数 secret ballot 無記名投票 動①投票する ②くじで決める
- □ **bamboo** 名竹類，竹，竹材 形竹の
- □ **ban** 名禁止，禁制 動禁止する
- □ **bar** 名①酒場，飲み屋 ②棒，かんぬき ③障害(物) 動～をかんぬきで閉める
- □ **base** 名基礎，土台，本部 動基礎を～に置く
- □ **baseball** 名①野球 ②野球用のボール
- □ **basement** 名地下(室)，基部
- □ **basic** 形基礎の，基本の 名《-s》基礎，基本，必需品
- □ **bathroom** 名トイレ，浴室
- □ **batter** 動①乱打する ②(人を)こきおろす 名①打者 ②(天ぷらなどの)衣
- □ **battle** 名戦闘，戦い 動戦う
- □ **bay** 名湾，入り江
- □ **BC** 名紀元前《before Christの略》
- □ **bean** 名豆
- □ **beauty** 名①美，美しい人［物］ ②《the –》美点
- □ **bedroom** 名寝室
- □ **beef** 名①牛肉 ②筋肉，強さ
- □ **beer** 名ビール
- □ **beginner** 名初心者
- □ **behind** 前①～の後ろに，～の背後に ②～に遅れて，～に劣って 副①後ろに，背後に ②遅れて，劣って
- □ **belong** 動《– to》～に属する，～のものである
- □ **Big Ben** 名ビッグベン《イギリスにある時計塔》
- □ **bill** 名①請求書，勘定書 ②法案 ③紙幣 ④ビラ 動①～に請求書を送る ②～を勘定書に記入する
- □ **birth** 名①出産，誕生 ②生まれ，起源，(よい)家柄
- □ **birthrate** 名出生率
- □ **bit** 名①《a – of》少しの～，1つの～ ②小片 **a bit** 少し，ちょっと 動 bite (～をかむ)の過去，過去分詞
- □ **bitter** 形①にがい ②つらい 副①にがく ②ひどく，激しく 名《the -(s)》①にがさ ②苦しみ
- □ **blanket** 名毛布 動～を毛布でくるむ

WORD LIST

- **blood** 名①血, 血液 ②血統, 家柄 ③気質
- **bloom** 名①花, 開花 ②若さ 動咲く[咲かせる]
- **blossom** 名花 動開花する
- **board** 名①板, 掲示板 ②委員会, 重役会 board of directors 重役[取締役]会 動～に乗り込む
- **boil** 動①沸騰する[させる], 煮える[煮る] ②激高する 名沸騰
- **bookstore** 名書店
- **boss** 名上司, 親方, 監督
- **bouquet** 名①花束 ②ほめ言葉
- **branch** 名①枝 ②支流 ③部門
- **brand-name** 名ブランド品, 商標名
- **Brazil** 名ブラジル《国名》
- **Brazilian** 名ブラジル人 形ブラジル人の, ブラジルの
- **bride** 名花嫁, 新婦
- **bridegroom** 名花婿, 新郎
- **briefly** 副①簡潔に ②少しの間
- **Britain** 名(Great Britainの略称)大ブリテン(島)
- **British** 形イギリスの British House of Lords 名英貴族院
- **bruise** 動①(人や果物に)傷をつける ②(感情などを)傷つける 名打撲傷
- **bubble** 名泡 動泡立つ, 沸き立つ
- **buckwheat** 名①そば, その実 ②そば粉
- **Buddha** 名仏陀, 釈迦(仏教の開祖)
- **Buddhism** 名仏教
- **Buddhist** 名仏教徒 形仏教(徒)の, 仏陀の
- **budget** 名①経費 ②予算 動予算を立てる
- **bullet train** 名新幹線
- **businessman** 名ビジネスマン, 実業家

C

- **cabbage** 名キャベツ
- **cabinet** 名①飾り棚 ②《C-》内閣, 閣僚 Cabinet Office 内閣府
- **calendar** 名カレンダー
- **California** 名カリフォルニア《地名》
- **camp** 名①野営(地), キャンプ ②収容所 動野営する, キャンプする
- **campaign** 名①キャンペーン(活動, 運動) ②政治運動, 選挙運動 ③軍事行動 動①従軍する ②運動に参加する
- **Canada** 名カナダ《国名》
- **candidate** 名①立候補者 ②学位取得希望者 ③志願者
- **candle** 名ろうそく
- **capital** 名①首都 ②大文字 ③資本(金) 形①資本の ②首都の ③最も重要な ④大文字の
- **career** 名①(生涯の, 専門的な)職業 ②経歴, キャリア
- **Caribbean Sea** 名カリブ海《地名》
- **carp streamer** 名こいのぼり
- **carriage** 名①馬車 ②乗り物, 車 ③車両
- **cartoon** 名①(時事風刺)マンガ ②アニメ映画 動マンガ化する
- **carved** 動carve(彫る, 彫刻する)の過去, 過去分詞
- **carving** 名彫刻, 彫刻作品
- **cash** 名現金(払い) 動～に現金で支払う, ～を換金する
- **cast** 動①投げる ②役を与える 投じる 名①投げること ②配役
- **casual** 形①偶然の ②略式の, カジュアルな ③おざなりの
- **catch a cold** 熟風邪をひく
- **CD** 名Compact Discの略, シィーディー

Japan FAQ

- **ceiling** 名 天井
- **celebrate** 動 ①祝う, 祝福する ②祝典を開く
- **celebration** 名 ①祝賀 ②祝賀会
- **celebrity** 名 ①有名人, 名士 ②名声
- **central** 形 中央の, 主要な
- **ceramic** 名 ①《通例-s》陶磁器 ②陶芸
- **ceremony** 名 ①儀式, 式典 ②礼儀, 作法, 形式ばること
- **certainly** 副 ①確かに, 必ず ②《返答に用いて》そのとおり, 承知しました
- **certificate** 名 ①証明書 ②免許状 動 証明書を与える
- **challenge** 名 ①挑戦 ②課題, 難問, 努力目標 動 ①挑戦する ②喚起する ③異議を唱える
- **chapter** 名 《書物の》章
- **charge** 動 ①《代金》を請求する ②《…を》~に負わせる 名 ①請求金額, 料金 ②責任 ③非難, 告発 in charge of~ ~を管理している, 任されている
- **check in** 熟 搭乗《宿泊》手続きする, チェックイン
- **cherry** 名 サクランボ, 桜
- **cherry blossom** 名 桜の花 cherry blossom front 桜前線
- **china** 名 ①陶磁器, 瀬戸物 ②《C-》中国
- **Chinese** 形 中国の, 中国人の 中国人, 中国語
- **Christian** 名 キリスト教信者 形 キリスト教の, キリスト教を信じる
- **Christianity** 名 キリスト教, キリスト教信仰《精神》
- **Christmas** 名 クリスマス
- **circle** 名 ①円, 円周 ②循環, 軌道 ③仲間, サークル 動 旋回する, 囲む
- **citizen** 名 ①市民, 国民 ②住民, 民間人
- **city hall** 名 市(区)役所
- **civil** 形 ①一般人の, 民間(人)の ②国内の, 国家の ③礼儀正しい civil war 内戦, 内乱
- **clan** 名 ①氏族 ②一家, 一門
- **classic** 形 古典的な, 伝統的な 名 古典
- **classical** 形 古典の, クラシックの
- **clear** 形 ①はっきりした, 明白な ②澄んだ ③《よく》晴れた 動 ①~をはっきりさせる ②~を片づける ③晴れる 副 ①はっきりと ②すっかり, 完全に
- **clearly** 副 ①明らかに, はっきりと ②《返答に用いて》そのとおり
- **client** 名 依頼人, 顧客, クライアント
- **climate** 名 気候, 風土, 環境
- **clinic** 名 診療所, クリニック
- **closely** 副 ①密接に ②念入りに, 詳しく ③ぴったりと
- **clothes** 名 衣服, 服装
- **co-worker** 名 同僚, 仕事仲間
- **coach** 名 ①長距離用のバス ②《鉄道の》普通客車 ③大型四輪馬車 ④コーチ, 指導員
- **coast** 名 海岸, 沿岸 動 滑降する, ~の沿岸を航行する
- **colleague** 名 同僚
- **collection** 名 収集, 収蔵品
- **colorful** 形 ①カラフルな, 派手な ②生き生きとした
- **combine** 動 ①結合する[させる] ②連合する, 協力する 名 合同, 連合
- **come into being** 熟 設立される
- **comedy** 名 ①喜劇 ②喜劇の場面
- **comfortable** 形 快適な, 心地いい
- **comic-strip** 名 《新聞・雑誌の》続きマンガ
- **Coming-of-Age Day** 名 成人の日

Word List

- **commemorate** 動①祝う, 記念する ②賛美する
- **commission** 名手数料, 委託, 委託
- **commoner** 名一般の人, 平民
- **commonly** 副一般に, 通例
- **communication** 名伝えること, 伝導, 連絡, コミュニケーション
- **commute** 動①通勤する ②定期券を買う ③一時払いにする
- **compare** 動①〜を比較する, 〜を対照する ②〜にたとえる (as) compared with 〜 〜と比較して, 〜に比べれば
- **compete** 動①競争する ②(競技に)参加する
- **competition** 名競争, 競合, コンペ
- **complain** 動①不平[苦情]を言う, ぶつぶつ言う ②(病状など)を訴える
- **complete** 形完全な, 全くの, 完成した 動〜を完成させる
- **completely** 副完全に, すっかり
- **complicated** 形①複雑な ②難しい, 困難な
- **compulsory** 形①強制的な ②義務の, 必修の
- **concern** 動①〜に関係する ②《受身形で》〜を心配する, 〜を気にする 名①関心事 ②関心, 心配 ③関係, 重要性
- **concert** 名①音楽[演奏]会, コンサート ②一致, 協力
- **condition** 名①(健康)状態, 境遇 ②《-s》状況, 様子 ③条件 動〜を適応させる, 〜を条件づける
- **confident** 形自信のある, 自信に満ちた
- **congested** 形詰め込まれた, 混雑した
- **connect** 動つながる[つなぐ], 《受身または – oneself》関係がある
- **consider** 動①考慮する ②(〜と)みなす ③〜を気にかける, 思いやる
- **consist** 動①《– of》(部分・要素)から成る ②《– in》〜に存在する, 〜にある
- **constituency** 名①選挙民, 後援者 ②選挙区
- **constitution** 名①憲法, 規約 ②構成, 構造
- **constitutional** 形①憲法の, 合憲の ②体質の constitutional monarchy 立憲君主国
- **construction** 名構造, 建設, 工事, 建物
- **consumption tax** 名消費税
- **contain** 動①〜を含む, 〜が入っている ②(感情など)を抑える
- **container** 名①容器, 入れ物 ②(輸送用)コンテナ
- **continent** 名①大陸, 陸地 ②《the C-》ヨーロッパ大陸
- **control** 動①〜を管理[支配]する ②〜を抑制する 名①管理, 支配(力) ②抑制
- **convenience store** 名コンビニエンスストア
- **convenient** 形便利な, 好都合な
- **conversation** 名会話, 会談
- **conveyor belt** 名ベルトコンベアー
- **cookie** 名クッキー
- **cooperation** 名①協力, 協業 ②協同組合
- **copy** 名①コピー ②(書籍の)一部, 冊 ③広告文 動〜を写す, まねる
- **corn** 名とうもろこし, 穀物
- **correct** 形正しい, 適切な, りっぱな 動(誤り)を訂正する, 〜を直す
- **corrupt** 形①堕落した ②不純な ③不正な 動①堕落させる ②買収する
- **corruption** 名①堕落 ②腐敗, 汚職
- **cosmetic** 名《-s》化粧品 形美容

の, 表面的な
- **cost** 名①値段, 費用 ②損失, 犠牲 動(金, 費用)がかかる, ～を要する
- **costume** 名衣装, 服装
- **count** 動①～を数える ②～を(…と)みなす ③重要[大切]である 名計算, 総計, 勘定
- **countryside** 名地方, 田舎
- **couple** 名①2つ, 対 ②夫婦, 一組, カップル ③2つ3つ, 数個
- **court** 名①中庭, コート ②法廷, 裁判所 ③宮廷, 宮殿
- **cover** 動①～をおおう, ～を包む, ～を隠す ②～を扱う, ～にわたる ③代わりを務める 名おおい, カバー
- **craftsman** 名職人, 熟練工
- **cram school** 名(日本の)塾
- **create** 動～を創造する, ～を生み出す, ～を引き起こす
- **creed** 名①(宗教上の)信条 ②信条, 信念
- **cremate** 動火葬する
- **crime** 名①(法律上の)罪, 犯罪 ②悪事, よくない行為
- **crimson** 形①濃赤色の ②血なまぐさい
- **crowded** 形混雑した, 満員の 動 crowd (群がる, 混雑する)の過去, 過去分詞
- **crown** 名①冠 ②頂, 頂上 ③《C-》王権, 王位, 国王 動戴冠する
- **cuisine** 名料理, 料理法
- **cure** 名治療, 治癒, 矯正 動～を治療する, ～を矯正する, ～をとり除く
- **current** 形現在の, 目下の, 通用[流通]している 名流れ, 電流, 風潮
- **currently** 副現在は, 今は
- **curse** 動～をのろう, ～をののしる 名のろい(の言葉), 悪態
- **custom** 名習慣, 慣例, 風俗
- **customer** 名顧客, お客

- **cutlet** 名カツレツ
- **cyclone** 名サイクロン, 大竜巻 **tropical cyclone** 熱帯低気圧

D

- **daily** 形毎日の, 日常の 副毎日, 日ごとに 名《-lies》日刊新聞
- **damage** 名損害, 損傷 動～に損害を与える, ～をそこなう
- **daytrip** 名日帰り旅行
- **deal** 動①～を分配する ②《– with [in]》～を扱う 名①取引, 扱い ②(不特定の)量, 額
- **dealt** 動 deal (～を分配する)の過去, 過去分詞
- **death** 名①死, 死ぬこと ②《the –》終えん, 消滅
- **debate** 動①討論する ②思案する 名討論, ディベート
- **debt** 名①借金, 負債 ②恩義, 借り
- **decision** 名①決心 ②決定, 判決 ③決断(力)
- **decorate** 動飾る, 装飾する
- **decoration** 名装飾, 飾りつけ
- **decrease** 動減少する 名減少
- **deep-fry** 動多めの油で揚げる
- **defeat** 動①～を打ち破る ②～をだめにする 名①敗北 ②挫折
- **define** 動定義する, 限定する
- **delicate** 形①繊細な, 壊れやすい ②淡い ③敏感な, デリケートな
- **delivery** 名①配達, ～便 ②譲渡, 交付 ③出産
- **democratic** 形①民主主義の, 民主制の ②民主的な
- **Democratic Party of Japan** 名民主党
- **department** 名①部門, 課, 局, 担当分野 ②《D-》(米国・英国の)省
- **depend** 動《– on [upon]》①～を

Word List

頼る, 〜をあてにする ②〜による

- **deposit** 動①置く ②預金する ③手付金を払う 名預金, 手付金
- **derail** 動脱線する
- **descendant** 名子孫, 末裔,(祖先からの)伝来物
- **descendent** 形①下降した ②世襲の, 先祖伝来の 名子孫, 末えい
- **descent** 名下り坂, 下降
- **design** 動〜を設計する, 〜を企てる 名デザイン, 設計(図)
- **designate** 動①示す ②〜と称する ③〜を指名する, 指定する
- **designer** 名デザイナー
- **despite** 前〜にもかかわらず
- **dessert** 名デザート
- **destination** 名行き先, 目的地
- **destroy** 動〜を破壊する, 〜を絶滅させる, 〜を無効にする
- **develop** 動①発達する[させる] ②〜を開発する developed countries 先進国
- **diarrhea** 名下痢
- **dictionary** 名辞書, 辞典
- **diet** 名①《the D-》国会, 議会 ②規定食, ダイエット, (日常の)飲食物 動規定食をとる[とらせる], 減食する[させる]
- **differently** 副〜と異なって, 違って
- **difficulty** 名①難しさ ②難局, 支障, 苦情, 異議 ③《-ties》財政困難
- **dine** 動食事をする, ごちそうする
- **dip** 動①ちょっと浸す, さっとつける ②(値段などが)下がる 名ちょっと浸すこと, (スープなどの)ひとすくい
- **diplomacy** 名外交
- **diplomat** 名外交官
- **direct** 形まっすぐな, 直接の, 率直な 副まっすぐに, 直接に 動①〜を指導する, 〜を監督する ②(目・注意・努力など)を向ける
- **directly** 副①じかに ②まっすぐに ③ちょうど
- **director** 名管理者, 指導者, 監督
- **disappear** 動見えなくなる, 姿を消す, なくなる
- **disappoint** 動〜を失望させる, 《受身形で》がっかりする, 失望する
- **disaster** 名災害, 災難, 全くの失敗
- **disk** 名《=disc》①円盤 ②(コンピューターの)ディスク
- **discount** 名ディスカウント, 割引 動割引する, 軽視する discount store ディスカウントストア
- **discussion** 名討議, 討論
- **display** 動飾る, 〜を展示する, 〜を示す 名展示, 陳列, 表出
- **disposable income** 名可処分所得, 手取り収入
- **distance** 名距離, 隔たり, 遠方
- **district** 名地区, 区域
- **distinct** 形①独特な ②はっきりした
- **divide** 動分かれる[分ける], 割れる[割る]
- **diving** 名ダイビング
- **division** 名①分割 ②部門 ③境界
- **divorce** 動離婚する 名離婚, 分離
- **document** 名書類, 文書, 資料 動〜を文書化する, 記録する
- **domestic** 形①家庭の ②国内の, 自国の, 国産の
- **donate** 動寄付する, 贈与する
- **doorway** 名戸口, 玄関, 出入り口
- **dough** 名練り粉, パン生地
- **Douglas MacArthur** 名ダグラス・マッカーサー《米陸軍元帥》
- **dozen** 名1ダース, 12(個) dozens of 〜 多数の〜
- **Dr.** 名〜博士,《医者に対して》〜先生

- **drama** 名劇, 演劇, ドラマ, 劇的な事件
- **dried** 形乾燥した 動dry (乾燥する[させる])の過去, 過去分詞
- **driver** 名①運転手 ②(馬車の)御者
- **drove** 動drive (車で行く, 運転する)の過去
- **dumpling** 名①ダンプリング《小麦粉を練っただんご》②ギョウザ
- **duty** 名①義務(感), 責任 ②職務, 任務 ③関税
- **dynasty** 名王朝(王家), その統治期間

E

- **earn** 動①(金)を儲ける, 稼ぐ ②(名声)を博す
- **earthquake** 名地震, 大変動
- **easily** 副①容易に, たやすく, 苦もなく ②気楽に
- **eastern** 形①東の, 東にある ②東洋の, 東洋風の
- **eat out** 熟外食する
- **economic** 形経済学の, 経済上の
- **economy** 名経済, 財政, 節約
- **edge** 名①刃 ②端, 縁 動①~に刃をつける, ~を鋭くする ②~を縁どる, 縁に沿って進む
- **education** 名教育, 教養
- **educator** 名教育者
- **Eiffel Tower** 名エッフェル塔《パリにある塔》
- **elderly** 形年配の, 初老の
- **elect** 動~を選ぶ, ~することに決める, 選挙する 形選ばれた
- **election** 名選挙, 投票
- **electoral** 形選挙の
- **electronic** 形電子工学の, エレクトロニクスの electronic product 電気製品
- **elegant** 形上品な, 優雅な
- **elementary** 形①初歩の ②単純な, 簡単な elementary school 小学校
- **embarrass** 動恥ずかしい思いをさせる, 困らせる
- **embarrassing** 形恥ずかしい, 厄介な
- **emigrate** 動移住する
- **emperor** 名《the-》皇帝, 天皇
- **employ** 動①(人)を雇う[使う] ②~を利用する 名雇用, 職業
- **employment** 名①雇用 ②仕事
- **empress** 名女帝, 皇后, 女王
- **encyclopedia** 名百科事典
- **enemy** 名敵
- **engineer** 名技師, 技術者
- **engineering** 名工学, 工業技術
- **England** 名①イングランド ②英国, イギリス
- **entertainment** 名①楽しみ, 娯楽 ②もてなし, 歓待
- **enthronement** 名即位(式)
- **entire** 形全体の, 完全な, 全くの
- **envelope** 名封筒, 包み
- **epicenter** 名(地震の)震央
- **equal** 形等しい, 均等な, 平等な 動~に匹敵する, 等しい
- **equinox** 名昼夜平分点
- **equipment** 名①準備 ②装備, 機器
- **era** 名時代, 年代
- **erupt** 動(火山が)噴火する, 噴出する, 爆発する, (戦争が)勃発する
- **establish** 動~を確立する, ~を立証する, ~を設置[設立]する
- **estimate** 動①見積もる ②評価する 名①見積(書) ②評価
- **etc.** 名~など, その他

WORD LIST

- **eternity** 名 永遠, 永久
- **Europe** 名 ヨーロッパ
- **European** 名 ヨーロッパ人 形 ヨーロッパ(人)の
- **European Union** 名 ヨーロッパ連合(EU)
- **everybody** 代 誰でも, 皆
- **everyone** 代 誰でも, 皆
- **everything** 代 すべてのこと[もの], 何でも, 何もかも
- **everywhere** 副 どこにいても, いたるところに
- **evil** 形 ①邪悪な ②有害な, 不吉な 名 ①邪悪 ②害, 災い, 不幸 副 悪く
- **exam** 名 テスト, 試験
- **except** 前 ～を除いて, ～のほかは except for ～ ～を除いて, ～がなければ 接 ～ということを除いて
- **executive** 形 ①実行の, 執行の ②行政の 名 ①高官, 実行委員 ②重役, 役員, 幹部
- **exercise** 名 ①運動, 体操 ②練習 動 運動, 練習する
- **existence** 名 存在, 実在, 生存
- **exotic** 形 異国風の, 魅惑的な, 外来の
- **expect** 動 ①～を予期[予測]する ②(当然のこととして)～を期待する
- **expedition** 名 遠征, 探検, 遠征[探検]隊
- **expense** 名 ①出費, 費用 ②犠牲, 代価
- **expert** 名 熟練した人, 専門家 形 ～に熟達した
- **explanation** 名 ①説明, 解説, 釈明 ②解釈, 意味
- **export** 動 輸出する 名 輸出, 国外への持ち出し
- **express** 動 ～を表現する, ～を述べる 形 ①明白な ②急行の 名 速達便, 急行列車 副 速達で, 急行で
- **expressway** 名 高速道路
- **extra** 形 ①余分の, 臨時の ②特別な 名 ①余分なもの ②エキストラ 副 余分に

F

- **factory** 名 工場, 製造所
- **fair** 形 ①正しい, 公平[正当]な ②快晴の ③色白の, 金髪の ④かなりの 副 ①公平に, きれいに ②みごとに
- **farmer** 名 農民, 農場経営者
- **farming** 名 農業(経営)
- **fashionable** 形 流行の, おしゃれな
- **fast-food** 形 ファーストフード専門の, 即席の
- **fat** 形 ①太った ②脂っこい ③分厚い 名 脂肪, 肥満
- **faq** 略 よくある質問 (= frequently asked questions)
- **fear** 名 ①恐れ ②心配, 不安 動 ①～を恐れる ②～を心配する
- **feature** 名 ①特徴, 特色 ②顔の一部, 《-s》顔立ち ③(ラジオ・テレビ・新聞などの)特集 動 ①～の特徴になる ②～を呼び物にする
- **fee** 名 謝礼, 料金 動 謝礼を払う
- **female** 形 女性の, 婦人の, 雌の 名 婦人, 雌
- **festival** 名 祭り, 祝日, ～祭
- **fever** 名 熱, 熱狂 動 ～を発熱させる, ～を熱狂させる
- **figure** 名 ①人(物)の姿, 形 ②図(形) ③数字 動 ①～を描写する, ～を想像する ②～を計算する ③目立つ, ～として現れる
- **film** 名 ①フィルム, 映画 ②膜 動 映画を製作[撮影]する
- **firefly** 名 ホタル
- **firework** 名 花火
- **fit** 形 ①適当な, 相応な ②体の調子がよい 動 合致[適合]する[させる]

Japan FAQ

- **flake** 名一片, 薄片
- **flavor** 名①風味, 味 ②趣 動風味を添える
- **float** 動①浮く, 浮かぶ ②(心に)浮かぶ 名浮くもの, いかだ
- **flooring** 名床張り
- **Florida** 名フロリダ《地名》
- **focus** 動(注意・関心などを)集中させる, ~に焦点を合わせる 名関心の的, 焦点, フォーカス
- **fool** 名ばか者, おろかな人 動~をばかにする, ~をだます, ふざける
- **force** 名力, 勢い 動~に強制する, 力づくで~する United States Forces 米軍
- **foreigner** 名外国人, 外国製品
- **form** 名①形, 形式 ②書式 動~を形づくる
- **former** 形①前の, 先の, 以前の ②《the-》(二者のうち)前者の
- **fortunately** 副幸運にも
- **France** 名フランス《国名》
- **freedom** 名①自由 ②束縛がないこと
- **French** 形フランス(人[語])の 名フランス語, 《the-》フランス人
- **friendly** 形親しみのある, 親切な, 友情のこもった 副友好的に, 親切に
- **fry** 動油で揚げる, いためる 名揚げ物, いため物
- **full-time** 名常勤の, 専任の
- **fully** 副十分に, 完全に, まるまる
- **funeral** 名葬式, 葬列 形葬式の
- **funny** 形①おもしろい, こっけいな ②奇妙な, うさんくさい
- **furthermore** 副さらに, そのうえ

G

- **gadget** 名機械装置, 小道具
- **gain** 動①~を得る, ~を増す ②進歩する, 進む 名①増加, 進歩 ②利益, 得ること, 獲得
- **gas stove** 名ガスストーブ
- **gasoline** 名ガソリン
- **gather** 動①集まる[集める] ②生じる, 増す ③~を推測する
- **GDP** 略国内総生産(gross domestic product)
- **general** 形①全体の, 一般の, 普通の ②おおよその 名大将, 将軍
- **generally** 副①一般に, だいたい ②たいてい
- **generation** 名世代, 同時代の人
- **genuine** 形①本物の ②心からの
- **geography** 名地理, 地理学
- **German-held** 形ドイツ占領下の
- **Germany** 名ドイツ
- **get along** 熟何とかやっていく, うまくやる
- **get around** 熟あちこち出歩く, 動き回る
- **get in the way of~** 熟~の行く手をふせぐ, ~の通り道に立つ
- **get one's hair cut** 熟散髪してもらう
- **ghost** 名幽霊
- **giant** 名①巨人, 大男 ②巨匠 形巨大な, 偉大な Giant Buddha 大仏
- **gift** 名①贈り物 ②(天賦の)才能 動~を授ける
- **global** 形①球状の ②地球規模の, 世界規模の, 広範囲の
- **goddess** 名女神
- **gold** 名金, 金貨, 金製品, 金色 形金の, 金製の, 金色の
- **golden** 副①金色の ②金製の ③貴重な Golden Week ゴールデンウィーク
- **golf** 名ゴルフ 動ゴルフをする
- **Goth** 名ゴス(黒を基調としたファ

WORD LIST

ッション。若者の間の流行)
- **gotten** 動 get (〜を得る)の過去分詞
- **government** 名 政治, 政府, 支配
- **grade** 名 学年, 等級, グレード 動 〜を格づけする
- **gradually** 副 だんだんと
- **graduate** 動 〜を卒業する 名 卒業生, (〜学校の)出身者
- **gram** 名 グラム《重さの単位》
- **grammar** 名 文法
- **Grand Canyon** 名 グランドキャニオン《地名》
- **granddaughter** 名 孫娘, 女の孫
- **grandparent** 名 祖父, 祖母
- **grave** 名 墓 形 重要な, 厳粛な, 落ち着いた
- **gravestone** 名 墓石
- **Great Hanshin Earthquake** 名 阪神淡路大震災
- **Great Kanto Earthquake** 名 関東大震災
- **greet** 動 ①(人)にあいさつする ②〜を(喜んで)迎える 名 《-ing》あいさつ(の言葉), あいさつ(状)
- **grower** 名 栽培者, 農場主
- **growth** 名 成長, 発展 形 成長している
- **grudge** 動 (物を)与えるのを惜しむ, 出ししぶる 名 恨み
- **Guam** 名 グアム《地名》
- **guarantee** 名 保証, 保証書, 保証人 動 保証する, 請け合う
- **guard** 名 ①警戒, 見張り ②番人 動 〜の番をする, 〜を監視する, 〜を守る
- **guest** 名 客, ゲスト
- **Gulf of Mexico** 名 メキシコ湾《地名》
- **gym** 名 ①体育館, ジム ②体育

H

- **habit** 名 習慣, 癖, 気質 in the habit of 〜 〜する習慣がある, 決まって〜する
- **Halloween** 名 ハロウィーン
- **hamburger** 名 ハンバーガー
- **handful** 名 一握り, 少量の
- **hang** 動 かかる[かける], 〜をつるす, ぶら下がる 名 かかり具合
- **happily** 副 幸福に, 楽しく, うまく, 幸いにも
- **happiness** 名 幸せ, 喜び, 幸運
- **hardly** 副 ①ほとんど〜でない, わずかに ②厳しく, かろうじて
- **harmony** 名 調和, 一致, ハーモニー
- **harvest** 名 ①収穫(物), 刈り入れ ②成果, 報い 動 (〜を)収穫する
- **Hawaii** 名 ハワイ《地名》
- **healthy** 形 健康な, 健全な, 健康によい
- **heat** 名 ①熱, 暑さ ②熱気, 熱意, 激情 動 (〜を)熱する, 暖める
- **heater** 名 ストーブ, 暖房器具
- **helpful** 形 役に立つ, 参考になる
- **hesitate** 動 ためらう, 躊躇する
- **high-fashion** 名 最新のファッション
- **high-quality** 形 質の高い
- **high-ranking** 形 地位の高い
- **highness** 名 《通常 His, Her, Your 〜》殿下
- **hiking** 名 ハイキング
- **hire** 動 ①〜を雇う ②〜を賃借りする 名 ①雇用 ②賃借り, 使用料
- **historical** 形 歴史的な
- **hobby** 名 趣味, 得意なこと
- **Hollywood** 名 ハリウッド《地名》
- **home-stay** 名 ホームステイ
- **homework** 名 宿題, 予習

- **honest** 形①正直な, 誠実な, 心からの ②公正な, 感心な
- **Hong Kong** 名香港《地名》
- **horror** 名①恐怖, ぞっとすること ②嫌悪 形恐怖の, ぞっとする
- **hostess** 名女主人, 女性司会者
- **hot spring** 名温泉
- **House of Councilors** 名参議院
- **House of Peers** 名貴族院
- **House of Representatives** 名衆議院
- **household** 名家庭, 世帯
- **housewife** 名主婦
- **however** 副たとえ～でも 接けれども, だが
- **humble** 形つつましい, 粗末な 動～をいやしめる, ～を謙虚にさせる
- **humid** 形湿った, むしむしする
- **hurricane** 名ハリケーン

I

- **ice cream** 名アイスクリーム
- **identity** 名①同一であること ②本人であること ③独自性
- **ignore** 動無視する, 怠る
- **illegal** 形違法な, 不法な
- **imbalance** 名不安定, 不釣り合い, アンバランス
- **imitation** 名①模倣, まね ②模造品
- **immediately** 副すぐに, ～するやいなや
- **immigrant** 名移民, 移住者 形移民に関する
- **imperial** 形①帝国の, 皇帝の, 皇后の ②荘厳なる Imperial Diet 帝国議会 imperial dynasty 王朝 Imperial Household Agency 宮内庁
- **import** 動輸入する 名輸入, 輸入品
- **impressive** 形印象的な, 深い感銘を与える
- **improve** 動改善する[させる], 進歩する
- **improvement** 名改良, 改善
- **in order to** 熟～するために
- **in the long run** 熟長い目で見れば, 結局は
- **include** 動①～を含む ②～を勘定に入れる
- **income** 名所得, 収入
- **incorporate** 動①合体させる, 組み入れる ②法人組織にする
- **increase** 動増加[増強]する[させる] 名増加(量), 増大
- **independent** 形独立した, 自立した
- **index** 名①索引 ②しるし, 指標
- **India** 名インド《国名》
- **indirect** 形間接的な, 二次的な
- **individual** 形独立した, 個性的な, 個々の 名①個体, 個人 ②人
- **industrialized countries** 名先進工業国
- **industry** 名産業, 工業, ～業
- **influence** 名影響, 勢力 動～に影響をおよぼす
- **ingredient** 名成分, 原料, 材料
- **injured** 形負傷した, (名誉・感情などを)そこねられた 動injure(痛める, 傷つける)の過去, 過去分詞
- **inn** 名①宿屋 ②居酒屋
- **inner** 形①内部の ②心の中の
- **instant** 形即時の, 緊急の, 即席の 名瞬間, 寸時
- **instead** 副その代わりに instead of ～ ～の代わりに, ～をしないで
- **institute** 動①制定する ②(調査を)実施する 名協会, 研究所

WORD LIST

- **Institute for Free Time Design** (財)自由時間デザイン協力会
- **insurance** 名保険
- **intense** 形①強烈な, 激しい ②感情的な
- **intensity** 名強烈さ, 激しさ
- **interestingly** 副おもしろく, (文を修飾して)おもしろいことに
- **International Date Line** 名国際日付変更線
- **internationally** 副国際的に
- **introduction** 名紹介, 導入
- **investigate** 動〜を研究する, 調査する, 捜査する
- **involve** 動①〜を含む, 伴う ②巻き込む, かかわらせる
- **isolation** 名孤立, 隔離 national isolation 鎖国
- **issue** 名①問題, 論点 ②発行物 ③出口, 流出 動①(〜から)出る, 生じる ②〜を発行する
- **Italian** 名イタリア人, イタリア語 形イタリアの
- **Italy** 名イタリア
- **item** 名①項目, 品目 ②(新聞などの)記事

J

- **Jacksonville** 名ジャクソンビル《地名》
- **Japan Sea** 名日本海
- **Japanese** 名日本人(語) 形日本の, 日本製の, 日本人(語)の
- **Japanese-style** 名日本式
- **jewelry** 名宝石, 宝飾品類
- **jogging** 名ジョギング
- **journey** 名①(遠い目的地への)旅 ②行程
- **judge** 動(〜に)判決を下す, 裁く, 判断する 名裁判官, 判事, 審査員
- **judicial** 形裁判(官)の, 司法の

K

- **keep up with** 熟〜に遅れずについていく
- **kerosene** 名灯油
- **kidnap** 動誘拐する 名誘拐
- **kilometer** 名キロメートル《長さの単位》
- **kindergarten** 名幼稚園
- **kindness** 名親切(な行為), 優しさ
- **Korea** 名韓国《国名》
- **Korean** 形朝鮮(韓国)の, 朝鮮(韓国)人(語)の 名朝鮮(韓国)人
- **kph** 名キロメートル/時《単位》

L

- **labor** 名労働, 骨折り 動①働く, 努力する, 骨折る ②苦しむ, 悩む labor force 労働力(人口)
- **lacquerware** 名漆器
- **land-use fee** 名土地使用料
- **landlord** 名①(男の)家主, 地主 ②パブの主人
- **lantern** 名手提げランプ, 灯篭
- **lasagna** 名ラザニア《料理名》
- **lately** 副近ごろ, 最近
- **latitude** 名緯度
- **leadership** 名指揮, リーダーシップ
- **league** 名①同盟, 連盟 ②《スポーツ》競技連盟
- **least** 形一番小さい, 最も少ない 副一番小さく, 最も少なく 名最小[少] at least 少なくとも
- **legislative** 形立法上の, 立法機関の

Japan FAQ

- **legislature** 名 立法府
- **leisure** 名 余暇, 自由時間
- **lemon** 名 レモン
- **less** 形 ～より小さい[少ない], 劣った 副 ～より少なく, ～ほどでなく 名 より少ない数[量・額]
- **level** 名 ①水平, 平面 ②水準 形 ①水平の, 平たい ②同等[同位]の 動 ①～を水平にする ②～を平等にする
- **Liberal Democratic Party** 名 自由民主党
- **lifespan** 名形 寿命(の)
- **lifestyle** 名 ライフスタイル, 生活様式
- **likely** 形 ①ありそうな, ～しそうな ②適当な 副 たぶん, おそらく
- **list** 名 名簿, 目録, 一覧表 動 ～を名簿[目録]に記入する
- **literacy** 名 読み書き能力
- **literature** 名 文学, 文芸
- **living expenditure** 名 消費支出
- **locate** 動 ①～に置く ②居住する[させる] ③位置する
- **location** 名 位置, 場所
- **longitude** 名 経度
- **look forward to** 熟 ～を楽しみに待つ, 期待する
- **loose** 形 自由な, ゆるんだ, あいまいな 動 ～をほどく, ～を解き放つ
- **lord** 名 首長, 主人, 領主
- **lot** 名 ①くじ ②運命 ③区画 vacant lot 空地
- **loudspeaker** 名 拡声器
- **lover** 名 ①愛人, 恋人 ②愛好者
- **lower** 形 も ①(～より)低い ②劣った, 下等の ③下部の, 下方の 動 ～を下げる, ～を低くする
- **lower-paid** 形 賃金の安い
- **loyal** 形 忠実な, 誠実な 名 忠実, 愛国者
- **luckily** 副 運よく, 幸いにも
- **lunar** 形 月の, 月面の lunar calendar 太陰暦
- **luxurious** 形 ぜいたくな, 豪華な, 最高級の

M

- **mad** 形 ①気の狂った ②逆上した, 理性をなくした ③ばかげた ④(～に)熱狂[熱中]して, 夢中の
- **magic** 名 ①魔法, 手品 ②魔力
- **magnitude** 名 マグニチュード《単位》
- **main** 形 主な, 主要な
- **mainly** 副 主に
- **maintain** 動 ①～を維持する ②～を養う
- **maintenance** 名 ①維持, 保存 ②整備
- **majesty** 名 ①威厳, 壮麗さ ②《M-》陛下
- **major** 形 ①大きいほうの, 主な, 一流の ②年長[古参]の 名 ①陸軍少佐 ②専攻科目 動 ～を専攻する
- **majority** 名 ①大多数, 大部分 ②過半数
- **male** 形 男の, 雄の 名 男, 雄
- **Malta** 名 マルタ《国名》
- **manager** 名 経営者, 支配人, 支店長, 部長
- **Manchuria** 名 満州《地名》
- **manufacturer** 名 製造業者, メーカー
- **manufacturing** 名 製作, 加工 形 製造の, 加工の
- **marriage** 名 結婚(生活[式])
- **marry** 動 (～と)結婚する
- **martial** 形 ①戦争の, 戦争に適した ②軍人らしい, 勇ましい martial arts 格闘技

WORD LIST

- **mask** 名 面, マスク
- **massive** 形 ①巨大な, 大量の ②堂々とした
- **master** 名 主人, 雇い主, 師 動 ①～を修得する ②～の主となる
- **mat** 名 マット, 敷物
- **match** 名 ①試合, 勝負 ②相手, つり合うもの 動 ①～を(…と)勝負させる ②～と調和する, ～ととり合う
- **matchmaker** 名 ①試合の組み合わせを決める人 ②結婚仲介人 ③(非公式の)仲人
- **material** 形 ①物質の, 肉体的な ②不可欠な, 重要な 名 材料, 原料
- **Matthew C. Perry** 名 マシュー・C・ペリー《米の提督》
- **mattress** 名 敷き布団, マットレス
- **mature** 形 ①(果物などが)熟した ②成長した, 発達した ③分別のある
- **measure** 動 ①～を測る, ～の寸法がある ②～を評価する 名 ①寸法, 測定, 計量, 単位 ②程度, 基準
- **medal** 名 メダル gold medal 金メダル
- **media** 名 メディア, マスコミ, 媒体
- **memorial** 名 記念物, 記録 形 記念の, 追悼の
- **menu** 名 メニュー, 献立表
- **merchant** 名 商人, 貿易商
- **meter** 名 ①メートル《長さの単位》②計量器, 計量する人
- **method** 名 ①方法, 手段 ②秩序, 体系
- **mid** 形 中央の, 中間の
- **middle** 名 中間, 最中 形 中間の, 中央の Middle Ages 《歴史》中世 middle school 中学校
- **midtown** 名 町の中心(付近)
- **might** 助 ①～かもしれない ②～してもよい, ～できる
- **mild** 形 柔和な, 温和な, 口あたりのよい, マイルドな
- **mile** 名 ①マイル《長さの単位。1,609m》②《-s》かなりの距離
- **military** 形 軍隊[軍人]の, 軍事の 名 《the -》軍, 軍部
- **Milky Way** 名 天の川, 銀河
- **mind** 名 ①心, 精神 ②知性 動 ①～を嫌だと思う ②～に気をつける, ～を用心する
- **mineral** 名 鉱物, 鉱石 形 鉱物の
- **miniature** 名 ミニチュア, 小模型 形 小型の
- **minister** 名 ①大臣, 閣僚, 公使 ②聖職者
- **ministry** 名 ①内閣 ②(日本の)省 ③大臣職
- **Ministry of Agriculture, Forestry and Fisheries** 名 農林水産省
- **Ministry of Economy, Trade and Industry** 名 経済産業省
- **Ministry of Education, Culture, Sports, Science and Technology** 名 文部科学省
- **Ministry of Finance** 名 財務省
- **Ministry of Foreign Affairs** 名 外務省
- **Ministry of Health, Labour and Welfare** 名 厚生労働省
- **Ministry of Internal Affairs and Communications** 名 総務省
- **Ministry of Justice** 名 法務省
- **Ministry of Land, Infrastructure and Transport** 名 国土交通省
- **Ministry of the Environment** 名 環境省
- **minor** 形 ①少数の, 小さい[少ない]方の ②重要でない
- **moat** 名 堀
- **mobile** 形 移動しやすい, 携帯できる 名 携帯電話

- **model** 名①模型, 設計図 ②模範 形模範の, 典型的な
- **modern** 形現代[近代]の, 現代的な, 最近の 名現代人
- **monarchy** 名①君主政治 ②王室 Japanese monarchy 日本の皇室
- **monk** 名修道士, 僧
- **monkey** 名サル
- **Montreal** 名モントリオール《地名》
- **monument** 名記念碑
- **moon viewing** 名月見
- **moss** 名コケ《植物》
- **mostly** 副主として, 多くは, ほとんど
- **motivate** 動動機付ける, 刺激する
- **Mount Fuji** 名富士山
- **movement** 名①動き, 運動 ②《-s》行動 ③引越し ④変動
- **multi-colored** 形多色の, 色とりどりの
- **musician** 名音楽家
- **myth** 名神話

N

- **NAFTA** 名北米自由貿易協定(ナフタ)
- **narrow** 形①狭い ②限られた 動狭くなる[する]
- **nation** 名国, 国家,《the -》国民
- **national** 形国家[国民]の, 全国の National Diet 国会 national flag 国旗
- **native** 形①出生(地)の, 自国の ②(~に)固有の, 生まれつきの, 天然の 名(ある土地に)生まれた人
- **naval** 形海軍の
- **nay** 名否, いや
- **nearby** 形近くの, 間近の 副近くで, 間近で
- **necessary** 形必要な, 必然の 名《-s》必需品, 必需品
- **neighborhood** 名近所(の人々), 付近
- **neither** 形どちらの~も…でない 代(2者のうち)どちらも~でない 副《否定文に続いて》~も…しない
- **New Guinea** 名ニューギニア《地名》
- **newspaper** 名新聞(紙)
- **noble** 形気高い, 高貴な, りっぱな 名貴族
- **nominate** 動①指名する, 推薦する ノミネートする ②指定する
- **non-Japanese** 名形日本人でない(人)
- **non-smoker** 名非喫煙者
- **non-smoking** 形禁煙の
- **none** 代~の何も[誰も, 少しも]…ない
- **noodle** 名麺類, ヌードル
- **normal** 形普通の, 平均の, 標準的な 名平常, 標準, 典型
- **North Pacific Ocean** 名北太平洋
- **northeast** 名形北東(の), 北東部(の) 副北東に(へ)
- **northern** 形北の, 北向きの, 北からの
- **notable** 名著名人, 著名な事物 形注目に値する, 著名な, 重要な
- **note** 名①メモ, 覚書 ②注釈 ③注意, 注目 ④手形 動①~を書き留める ②~に注意[注目]する
- **notice** 名①注意 ②通知 ③公告 動①~に気づく, ~を認める ②~に通告する
- **noun** 名名詞
- **nowadays** 副この頃は, 現在では
- **nuclear** 形核の, 原子力の 名核兵器

WORD LIST

- **nursery** 名 ①育児室, 託児所 ②苗床, 養成所

O

- **object** 名 ①物, 事物 ②目的物, (研究の)対象 動 反対する, (〜に)異議を唱える
- **observe** 動 ①観察する ②〜に気づく ③(祝日などを)祝う
- **occasion** 名 ①場合, (特定の)時 ②機会, 好機 ③理由, 根拠
- **occupation** 名 ①職業, 仕事, 就業 ②占有, 居住, 占領 《the O-》軍隊による占領, 占拠
- **occur** 動 (事が)起こる, 生じる, (考えなどが)浮かぶ
- **ODA** 略 政府開発援助 (= Official Development Assistance)
- **OECD** 略 経済協力開発機構 (= Organization for Economic Cooperation and Development)
- **offer** 動 (〜を)申し出る, (〜を)申し込む, (〜を)提供する 名 提案, 提供 offer up 供える
- **offering** 名 ①供物 ②提供, 申し出
- **officer** 名 役人, 公務員, 警察官
- **oil** 名 ①油, 石油 ②油絵の具, 油絵
- **okay** 形 《許可, 同意, 満足などを表して》よろしい, 正しい 名 許可, 承認
- **Olympic** 形 オリンピックの the Olympic games オリンピック大会
- **on and off** 熟 断続して, (雨・雪が)降ったりやんだり
- **on time** 熟 時間どおりに
- **onto** 前 〜の上へ
- **open-air** 形 野外, 戸外
- **openly** 副 率直に, 公然と
- **opportunity** 名 好機, 適当な時期 [状況]
- **option** 名 ①選択 ②オプション, 選択可能な付属品
- **Organization for Economic Cooperation and Development** 名 経済協力開発機構 (OECD)
- **organize** 動 (〜を)組織する
- **origin** 名 起源, 出自
- **originally** 副 最初は, そもそもは
- **originate** 動 始まる[始める], 起こす, 生じる
- **Oscar** 名 オスカー(賞・像。米アカデミー賞で与えられる)
- **oven** 名 かまど, 天火, オーブン
- **overwork** 名 働きすぎ, オーバーワーク
- **overseas** 形 海外の, 外国への
- **overthrown** 形 倒した, 転覆した
- **overtime** 名形 残業, 時間外
- **owner** 名 持ち主, オーナー

P

- **Pacific Ocean** 名 太平洋
- **pack** 名 ①包み, 荷物 ②群れ, 一組 動 (〜を)荷造りする, 詰め込む
- **paid** 動 pay (〜を払う)の過去, 過去分詞 形 有給の, 支払いずみの
- **palace** 名 宮殿, 大邸宅
- **pamphlet** 名 小冊子, パンフレット
- **paradise** 名 ①天国 ②地上の楽園
- **parallel** 形 平行の, 平行して 名 平行線, 平行面, 類似
- **part-time** 形 パートタイムの, 非常勤の
- **participate** 動 参加する, 加わる
- **particularly** 副 特に, とりわけ
- **pass down** 熟 (次の世代に)伝える, 譲り渡す
- **passenger** 名 乗客, 旅客
- **passionate** 形 情熱的な, (感情が)

Japan FAQ

激しい, 短気な
- **past** 形過去の, この前の 名過去(の出来事) 前 (時間が)〜を過ぎて, 〜を越して 副通り越して, 過ぎて
- **paste** 名①のり, のり状のもの ②ペースト 練り粉 動のりで貼る
- **pastime** 名気晴らし, 娯楽
- **patient** 形我慢[忍耐]強い, 根気のある 名病人, 患者
- **pay** 動〜を支払う, 〜に報いる 名給料, 報い
- **payment** 名支払い(金)
- **Pearl Harbor** 名真珠湾《地名》
- **pebble** 名①小石 ②水晶
- **peninsula** 名半島
- **pension** 名年金 pension system 年金制度 動〜に年金を与える
- **per** 前〜につき, 〜ごとに
- **perform** 動①(任務などを)行なう[果たす], 実行する ②〜を演じる, 演奏する
- **performance** 名①実行, 行為 ②成績, できばえ ③演劇, 演奏
- **period** 名期, 期間, 時代 形時代物の
- **personal** 形①個人の ②本人自らの ③容姿の
- **personality** 名人格, 個性
- **personally** 副個人的には, 自分で
- **photograph** 名写真 動写真を撮る
- **phrase** 名句, 慣用句, 名言 動〜を言葉で言い表す
- **pickled** 形ピクルスにした
- **pickles** 名ピクルス Japanese pickles 漬物
- **pilgrimage** 名巡礼(の旅)
- **pine-tree** 名松の木
- **plate** 名①(浅い)皿, 1皿の料理 ②金属板, 標札 ③プレート《地質》
- **platform** 名プラットフォーム, 壇
- **play catch** 熟キャッチボールをする
- **player** 名①競技者, 選手, 演奏者, 俳優 ②演奏装置
- **pleated** 形プリーツの, ひだのある
- **plum** 名セイヨウスモモ, プラム, 梅
- **policy** 名①政策, 方針, 手段 ②保険証券
- **polite** 形ていねいな, 礼儀正しい, 洗練された
- **political** 形①政治(上)の ②国家の, 国政の ③政党の
- **politician** 名政治家, 政略家
- **politics** 名政治(学), 政策
- **popularity** 名人気, 流行
- **population** 名人口, 住民(数)
- **populous** 形人口の多い
- **pork** 名豚肉
- **portable** 形持ち運びのできる, ポータブルな
- **position** 名①位置, 場所 ②地位, 身分, 職 ③立場, 状況
- **positive** 形①明確な, 明白な ②確信している
- **possible** 形可能な, あり[起こり]得る
- **postal** 形郵便の, 郵送の
- **pot** 名つぼ, (深い)なべ 動〜をつぼに入れる, 〜をはち植えにする
- **potential** 名可能性, 潜在(性・能力), 素質 形可能性のある, 起こりえる, 潜在的な
- **pottery** 名陶器
- **pound** 動①すりつぶす, 粉々にする ②何度も強く打つ
- **powerful** 形力強い, 実力のある, 影響力のある
- **praise** 動〜をほめる, 〜を賞賛する 名賞賛
- **pray** 動祈る, 懇願する
- **predict** 動〜を予測する, 予言する

Word List

- **pref.** 略県, 府 (= prefecture)
- **prefecture** 名県, 府
- **prehistoric** 形①先史時代の ②時代遅れの
- **preserve** 動~を保存[保護]する, ~を保つ
- **press** 動①(~を)圧する, 押す ②(~を)強要する, ~に迫る 名①圧迫, 押し, 切迫 ②出版物[社], 新聞
- **previous** 形前の, 先の
- **price** 名①値段, 代価, 代償 ②《-s》物価, 相場
- **pride** 名誇り, 自慢, 自尊心 動~を誇る, ~を自慢する
- **prime minister** 名首相,(日本の)内閣総理大臣 Prime Minister's Office 総理府
- **prince** 名王子, 親王
- **princess** 名王女, 内親王
- **private** 形①私的な, 個人の ②民間の ③内密の, 人里離れた
- **probably** 副たぶん, あるいは
- **product** 名①製品, 産物 ②成果, 結果
- **professional** 形専門の, プロの, 職業的な 名専門家, プロ
- **professor** 名教授, 師匠
- **progress** 名①進歩, 前進 ②成り行き, 経過 動前進する, 上達する
- **prohibit** 動①禁止する ②~が…するのを妨げる
- **promotion** 名①昇進 ②促進 ③宣伝販売
- **pronounce** 動①発音する ②申し渡す
- **properly** 副適切に, きっちりと
- **property** 名①財産, 所有物[地] ②性質, 属性
- **proportional** 形比例した proportional representation 比例代表選挙
- **propose** 動①~を申し込む, ~を提案する ②結婚を申し込む
- **prosperity** 名繁栄, 繁盛
- **prostitute** 名売春婦
- **protein** 名タンパク質
- **provide** 動①~に…を供給する ②用意する,(~に)備える
- **pub** 名酒場
- **public bath** 名公衆浴場, 銭湯
- **publishing company** 名出版社
- **punch** 動げんこつでなぐる パンチする, 名パンチ, 一撃
- **purify** 動浄化する
- **purse** 名①財布, 小銭入れ ②小物入れ
- **put away** 熟片付ける, しまう

Q

- **qualification** 名①資格, 技能 ②資格証明書
- **quarter** 名①4分の1 ②15分 ③25セント(銀貨) 動~を4等分する
- **quickly** 副敏速に, 急いで

R

- **rabbit** 名①ウサギ(の毛皮) ②弱虫
- **radio** 名①ラジオ ②無線電話[電報] 動放送する
- **rail** 名①横木, 手すり ②レール, 鉄道
- **rainfall** 名降雨, 降雨量
- **raise** 動①~を上げる[高める] ②~を起こす ③~を育てる 名高める[上げる]こと, 昇給
- **range** 名列, 連なり, 範囲 動①並ぶ[並べる] ②~に及ぶ mountain range 山脈, 連山

- **rank** 名①列 ②階級, 位 ③《-ing》順位, 等級づけ 動①並ぶ［並べる］②〜を分類する 形《-ing》上位の, 一流の
- **rapid** 形 速い, 急な, すばやい
- **rate** 名①割合, 率 ②相場, 料金 動①〜を見積もる, 評価する［される］②〜に等級をつける
- **rather** 副①むしろ, かえって ②いくぶん, やや
- **ratify** 動 承認する, 批准する
- **raw** 形①生の, 未加工の ②未熟な 名 なまもの
- **re-create** 動 再現する, 作り直す
- **re-name** 動 名前を変える, 改名する
- **realistic** 形①現実的な ②写実的な
- **realize** 動①〜を理解する, 〜を悟る ②〜を実現する
- **rebuild** 動 再建する, 改造する
- **recent** 形 近頃の, 近代の
- **recently** 副 ついこのあいだ, 近頃
- **reception** 名①もてなし, 接待 ②宴会 ③受付
- **recognizable** 動 見覚えがある, 認識できる
- **recognize** 動 〜を認める, 〜を認識［承認］する
- **reconstruct** 動 再建する, 再現する
- **record** 名 記録, 登録, 履歴 **on record** 記録では, 公式に言明した 動 〜を記録［登録］する
- **recovery** 名 回復, 復旧, 立ち直り
- **refer** 動①〜に言及する, 触れる ②〜を参照する ③〜を表す
- **refined** 形 精製された, 上品な, 洗練された 動 refine（精製する）の過去, 過去分詞
- **reflect** 動 映る, 反響する, 反射する

- **reform** 動 改善する, 改革する 名 改善, 改良, 改革
- **region** 名①地方, 地域 ②範囲
- **regional** 形 地方の, 地方による
- **register** 動①登録（記録）する ②署名する ③書留にする 名 一覧表, 記録
- **regular** 形①いつもの, 通常の ②規則的な, 秩序のある, 習慣的な
- **regularly** 副 整然と, 規則的に
- **reheat** 動 温め直す
- **reign** 名①治世 ②君臨, 支配 動 君臨する, 支配する
- **relationship** 名①関係, 関連 ②血縁関係
- **relative** 形 関係のある, 相対的な 名 親戚, 同族
- **relax** 動 くつろぐ, ゆるめる
- **release** 動 解き放す, 〜を外す 名 解放, 釈放
- **religion** 名①宗教, 〜教 ②信条
- **religious** 形①宗教の ②信心深い
- **remade** 動 remake（〜を作り直す）の過去, 過去分詞
- **remain** 動①残っている, 残る ②〜のままである［いる］
- **remove** 動①〜を取り去る, 〜を除去する ②（衣類を）脱ぐ
- **rent** 動 〜を賃借りする 名 使用料, 賃貸料, 家賃
- **repair** 動 〜を修理する 名 修理
- **replaced** 動 replace（〜に取って代わる, 戻しておく）の過去, 過去分詞
- **reply** 動 答える, 返事をする, 応答する 名 答え, 返事, 応答
- **represent** 動①〜を表現する ②〜を意味する ③〜を代表する
- **representation** 名①表現 ②代表, 代理
- **reputation** 名 評判, 名声

Word List

- **require** 動①〜を必要とする，〜を要する ②〜を命じる，〜を請求する
- **requirement** 名必要なもの，必要条件
- **researcher** 名研究者
- **reserve** 動①とっておく，備えておく ②〜を予約する ③〜を留保する
- **resident** 名居住者，在住者
- **resort** 名行楽地，リゾート
- **respect** 名尊敬，尊重 動〜を尊敬[尊重]する
- **restrict** 動制限する
- **result** 名①結果，成り行き ②成績 動(結果として)起こる[生じる]，結局〜になる **as a result** 結果として
- **retail** 形小売りの 名小売り(店)
- **retainer** 名①保持者，保有者 ②従業員 ③家臣，家来
- **retired** 形退職した，引退した 動 retire (引き下がる，退職する)の過去，過去分詞
- **Richter scale** 名リヒタースケール《マグニチュードによる地震の規模を表す尺度》
- **right by** 熟〜のすぐそばで
- **ring** 名①輪，円形，指輪 ②競技場 動①〜を輪でとり囲む ②鳴る[鳴らす] ③〜に電話をかける **the Ring of Fire** 環太平洋火山帯
- **role** 名①(劇などの)役 ②役割，任務
- **root** 名①根，根元 ②根源，原因 ③《-s》先祖
- **route** 名道，道筋，ルート
- **ruler** ①支配者 ②(直)定規
- **rural** 形田舎の，地方の
- **rush** 動突進する，〜をせきたてる 名突進，突撃，殺到
- **Russia** 名ロシア《国名》
- **Russo-Japanese** 形ロシアと日本の **the Russo-Japanese War** 日露戦争

S

- **sacred** 形神聖な
- **safely** 副安全に，間違いなく
- **safety** 名安全，無事，確実
- **sailor** 名水夫，水兵，船員
- **Saipan** 名サイパン《地名》
- **salty** 形塩の，塩を含む
- **samurai** 名武士，侍
- **San Francisco Peace Treaty** 名サンフランシスコ講和条約
- **sauce** 名ソース
- **scale** 名①目盛り ②割合，程度 ③うろこ ④はかり 動〜をはかる
- **scandal** 名スキャンダル，醜聞
- **scary** 形恐ろしい，怖い
- **scenery** 名風景，景色
- **schedule** 名予定，スケジュール 動予定を立てる
- **scholar** 名学者
- **school** 名①学校 ②学派，流派
- **score** 名①(競技の)得点，スコア，(試験の)点数 ②きざみ目 ③総楽譜 動(競技で)得点する，(〜を)採点する
- **scream** 名金切り声，絶叫 動叫ぶ，金切り声を出す
- **scroll** 名巻物，古文書 動(コンピュータで)スクロールする **hanging scroll** かけ軸
- **sculpture** 名①彫刻 ②彫刻作品 動彫刻する
- **seafood** 名海産物，シーフード
- **seal** 名印，封印，印鑑
- **seaside** 名海辺，海岸，浜
- **seasonal** 形季節の
- **seat of** 熟〜の所在地，〜のお膝下

Japan FAQ

- **seaweed** 名海藻
- **secret** 形①秘密の, 隠れた ②神秘の, 不思議な 名秘密
- **secure** 形①安全な ②しっかりした, 保証された 動①~を安全にする ②~を確保する, ~を手に入れる
- **seem** 動~に見える, ~のように思われる
- **seldom** 副まれに, めったに~ない
- **select** 動~を選択する 形選んだ, 一流の, えりぬきの
- **self-introduction** 名自己紹介
- **senior** 形①年長の, 年上の ②古参の ③上級の 名年長者, 先輩, 先任者
- **sense** 名①感覚 ②《-s》正気, 本性 ③常識, 分別 ④意味 動~を感じる
  make sense なるほどと思える, 筋が通っている
- **sensitive** 形敏感な, 感度がいい, 繊細な
- **separate** 動 分離[分割]する[させる], 別れる[別れさせる] 形分かれた, 別れた
- **separation** 名分離(点), 離脱, 分類
- **series** 名一続き, 連続, シリーズ
- **serious** 形①まじめな, 真剣な ②重大な, 深刻な ③(病気などが)重い
- **serve** 動①(~に)仕える, 奉仕する ②(客の)応対をする, (~に)給仕する ③(役目を)果たす, 勤める
- **service** 名①勤務, 業務 ②公益事業 ③点検, 修理 動~の修理をする
- **sesame** 名ゴマ
- **sex** 名性, 性別, 男女
- **shake** 動①~を振る, 揺れる[揺さぶる] ②~を動揺させる 名振ること
- **shape** 名①形, 姿, 型 ②状態, 調子 動~を形作る, ~を具体化する
- **sheet** 名①シーツ ②(紙などの)1枚

- **shindo scale** 名震度スケール《震度で地震の規模を表す尺度》
- **shellfish** 名貝, 甲殻類《カニ, エビなど》
- **shogunate** 名将軍職, 幕府
- **shown** 動 show (~を見せる)の過去分詞
- **shred** 名切れ端, 断片 動細く切る
- **shrine** 名神社, 廟, 聖堂
- **shy** 形内気な, 恥ずかしがりの, 臆病な
- **Siberia** 名シベリア《地名》
- **side** 名①側, 横, そば, 斜面 動味方する
- **sidewalk** 名歩道
- **sightseeing** 名観光, 見物
- **silver** 名銀, 銀貨, 銀色 形銀製の
- **similar** 形~に類似した, よく似た
- **simply** 副①簡単に ②単に, ただ
- **single** 形たった一つの, 独身の 名 (ホテルなどの)1人用の部屋, シングルス[単試合]
- **Sino-Japanese War** 名日清戦争
- **situation** 名①場所, 位置 ②状況, 境遇, 立場
- **ski** 名スキー, スキー板
- **skiing** 名スキー(をすること) **go skiing** スキーに行く
- **skill** 名①技能, 技術 ②上手, 熟練
- **skyscraper** 名超高層ビル
- **slice** 名薄切りの1枚, 部分 動~を薄く切る
- **slight** 形①わずかな ②ほっそりして ③とるに足らない
- **slightly** 副わずかに, いささか
- **slipper** 名①部屋ばき, スリッパ ②(車の)歯止め
- **slowly** 副遅く, ゆっくり
- **smoke** 動喫煙する, 煙を出す 名①煙, 煙状のもの ②《-ing》喫煙

WORD LIST

- **smoker** 名 喫煙家, 煙草を吸う人
- **smooth** 形 ①なめらかな ②円滑な 動 なめらかにする[なる]
- **snack** 名 軽食
- **sneeze** 動 ①くしゃみをする ②(〜を)鼻であしらう 名 くしゃみ
- **snowboarding** 名 スノーボード(をすること)
- **soccer** 名 サッカー
- **social** 形 ①社会の, 社会的な ②社交的な, 愛想のよい
- **socialize** 動 社交的に交際する, つき合う
- **softness** 名 柔らかさ, 柔軟, 優しさ
- **solve** 動 〜を解く, 〜を解決する
- **someone** 代 ある人, 誰か
- **something** 代 ①ある物, 何か ②いくぶん, 多少
- **sometime** 副 いつか, そのうち
- **sometimes** 副 ときどき
- **somewhere** 副 ①どこかへ[に] ②ある時, いつか, およそ
- **source** 名 源, 原因, もと
- **southern** 形 南の, 南向きの, 南からの
- **southwest** 名形 南西(の), 南西部(の)
- **souvenir** 名 おみやげ
- **sow** 動 (種子を)まく, まき散らす, 広める.
- **soy sauce** 名 しょうゆ
- **soybean** 名 大豆
- **spa** 名 鉱泉, 温泉
- **spaghetti** 名 スパゲッティ
- **Spanish** 形 スペインの 名 スペイン語[人]
- **speaker** 名 ①話す人, 演説者, 代弁者 ②スピーカー, 拡声器 ③議長
- **specialize** 動 専門にする
- **speed** 名 速力, 速度 動 急ぐ[急がせる]
- **spirit** 名 ①霊 ②精神, 気力
- **spirited away** 熟 神隠しに遭う
- **spot** 名 ①地点, 場所 ②斑点, しみ 動 〜に点を打つ, 〜にしみをつける
- **sq** 名 square (平方) の略《単位》
- **square** 名 ①正方形, 四角い広場, (市外の)一区画 ②2乗, 平方 形 ①正方形の, 四角な, 直角な, 角ばった ②平方の
- **squat** 動 しゃがむ 名 しゃがむこと
- **stability** 名 安定(性), 持続
- **staff** 名 職員, スタッフ
- **stair** 名 ①(階段の)1段 ②《-s》階段, はしご
- **stake** 名 棒 動 ①賭ける ②くいで囲む **stake out** 囲う, 仕切る
- **stall** 名 ①(馬小屋などの)仕切り ②屋台, 露店
- **stamp** 名 ①印 ②切手 動 ①〜に印を押す ②〜を踏みつける
- **staples** 名 ①くぎ, ホッチキスの針 ②主要産物, (必需)食料品
- **state** 名 ①有様, 状態 ②《the-》国家, (アメリカなどの)州 動 〜を述べる 形 国家の
- **stationery** 名 文房具
- **statue** 名 像 **Statue of Liberty** 自由の女神
- **status** 名 ①(社会的な)地位, 身分, 立場 ②状態
- **stay over** 熟 泊まる, 泊まりがけ
- **steak** 名 ステーキ
- **steal** 動 ①〜を盗む ②こっそり手に入れる[動く] 名 盗み, 盗品
- **stock** 名 ①貯蔵 ②仕入れ品, 在庫品 ③株式 動 仕入れする, 蓄える **Tokyo Stock Exchange** 東京証券取引所
- **stone** 名 石, 小石 形 石(製)の
- **storm** 名 嵐, 暴風雨 ②強襲 動 ①〜を襲撃[強襲]する ②嵐が吹く

Japan FAQ

- **Strait of Gibraltar** 名 ジブラルタル海峡《地名》
- **stranger** 名 ①見知らぬ人, 他人 ②不案内[不慣れ]な人
- **straw** 名 麦わら, わら
- **streamer** 名 吹き流し
- **strength** 名 ①力, 体力 ②長所, 強み ③強度, 濃度
- **stress** 名 ①圧迫 ②緊張, ストレス ③強調
- **string** 名 ①ひも, 糸, 弦 ②一連, 一続き 動 ～に糸[ひも]をつける
- **strip** 名 細長い1片, 切れ
- **strongly** 副 強く, がんじょうに, 猛烈に, 熱心に
- **stuck out** 熟 目立つ, 明瞭である
- **style** 名 やり方, 流儀, 様式, スタイル 動 ～と称する, ～に称号を授ける
- **subway** 名 ①地下鉄 ②地下道
- **succeed** 動 ①成功する ②(～の)跡を継ぐ
- **success** 名 ①成功, 幸運 ②上首尾
- **successful** 形 成功した, うまくいった
- **suggest** 動 ①～を暗示する ②～を提案する
- **suit** 名 ①スーツ ②訴訟 動 適合する[させる], 似合う
- **suitcase** 名 スーツケース
- **sun goddess** 名 太陽の女神
- **sunlight** 名 日光
- **support** 動 ①～を支える ②～を養う, ～を援助する 名 ①支え ②援助, 扶養
- **Supreme Commander** 名 最高司令官
- **surround** 動 ～を囲む, ～を包囲する
- **surrounding** 名 ①(-s)環境 ②周辺地域, 近郊
- **survey** 動 ①見渡す ②概観する ③調査する 名 ①概観 ②調査
- **survive** 動 生き残る, 何とかなる, ～を切り抜けて生きる
- **suspicious** 形 怪しい, 疑い深い
- **sweep** 動 ①～を掃く ②(風などが)吹き払う 名 掃くこと
- **sweet-bean-paste-filled** 形 あんの詰まった
- **sword** 名 ①剣, 刀 ②武力
- **syllable** 名 音節
- **symbol** 名 シンボル, 象徴

T

- **tableware** 名 食卓用食器類
- **Taiwan** 名 台湾《地名》
- **take care of** 熟 ～の世話をする
- **take over** 熟 占領する, 支配権を握る
- **take place** 熟 起る, 行なわれる
- **take up** 熟 (場所・時間を)取る
- **talent** 名 才能, 才能ある人
- **target** 名 標的, 目的物, 対象 動 ～を的[目標]にする
- **taste** 名 ①味, 風味 ②好み, 趣味 動 ～の味がする, (～を)味わう
- **tasty** 形 おいしい
- **tax** 名 ①税 ②重荷, 重い負担 動 ①～に課税する ②～に重荷を負わせる
- **technology** 名 技術, テクノロジー
- **teenager** 名 十代, ティーンエイジャー
- **Teheran** 名 テヘラン《地名》
- **television** 名 テレビ
- **temperature** 名 温度, 体温
- **temple** 名 寺, 神殿
- **territory** 名 ①領土 ②(広い)地域, 範囲, 領域

WORD LIST

- **theater** 名劇場
- **thick** 形厚い, 密集した, 濃厚な 名最も厚い[強い, 混んだ, 濃い]部分
- **thin** 形薄い, 細い, やせた, まばらな 動薄く[細く]なる[する]
- **throughout** 前～の至るところに 副初めから終わりまで
- **titanic** 形チタンの, タイタン神のような, 巨大な 名《T-》タイタニック号, 映画『タイタニック』
- **toilet** 名トイレ, 化粧室
- **toll expressway** 名有料高速道路
- **tool** 名道具, 用具, 工具
- **topic** 名話題, 見出し
- **total** 形総計の, 全体の, 完全な 名全体, 合計 動～を合計する
- **tour** 名ツアー, 見て回ること, 視察
- **tourism** 名観光旅行
- **tourist** 名旅行者
- **tournament** 名トーナメント
- **trade** 名取引, 貿易, 商業 動取引する, 貿易する, 商売する
- **trading** 名貿易, 通商
- **tradition** 名①伝統, しきたり ②伝説, 伝承
- **traditional** 形伝統的な
- **traditionally** 副伝統的に, もともとは
- **tragic** 形悲劇の, 痛ましい
- **trail** 名小道, (通った)跡 動～をひきずる, ～の跡を追う[つける]
- **trait** 名特色, 特徴
- **translate** 動翻訳する
- **translation** 名翻訳, 言い換え, 解釈
- **transportation** 名交通(機関), 輸送手段
- **treat** 動①～を取り扱う ②～を治療する ③おごる 名楽しみ
- **treaty** 名条約, 協定
- **triangle** 名三角形
- **tribe** 名部族, 一族
- **trick** 名①策略 ②いたずら, 冗談 ③手品, 錯覚 動～をだます **trick into** かつぐ
- **tried** 動 try (～しようと試みる)の過去, 過去分詞 形確実な, あてになる, 信頼できる
- **trousers** 名ズボン
- **truth** 名①真理, 事実, 本当 ②誠実, 忠実さ
- **Tsingtao** 名青島《地名》
- **tuition** 名①指導, 授業 ②授業料
- **tune** 名①曲, 節 ②正しい調子 動(ラジオ, テレビなどを)～に合わせる
- **tying** 動 tie (～を結ぶ, ～を縛る)の現在分詞
- **typhoon** 名台風
- **typical** 形典型的な, 象徴的な

U

- **U.S.** 名アメリカ合衆国 (=United States of America)
- **U.K.** 名 (グレートブリテンおよび北アイルランド) 連合王国, 英国
- **uncommon** 形珍しい, まれな
- **underneath** 前真下に(の, を) 副下に(を), 根底は
- **unemployment** 名失業
- **unfortunately** 副不幸にも, 運悪く
- **unfriendly** 形友情のない, 不親切な
- **unheard** 形聞こえない **unheard of** 今まで聞いたことがない
- **unify** 動～を一つにする, 統一する
- **unique** 形唯一の, ユニークな, 独自の
- **university** 名(総合)大学

- **unless** 接 もし~でなければ、~しなければ
- **unusual** 形 普通でない、珍しい、見[聞き]慣れない
- **upper gallery** 名 天井桟敷
- **upset** 形 憤慨して 動 気を悪くさせる
- **urban** 形 都会の、都会ふうの
- **used** 形 《be – to ~》~に慣れている
- **utility** 名 ①実用性 ②公共サービス《ガス、電気、水道など》

V

- **vacant** 形 空いている、使用されていない
- **value** 名 価値、値打ち、価格 動 ~を評価する、~に値をつける
- **variety** 名 ①変化、多様性、寄せ集め ②種類
- **vary** 動 変わる[変える]、~を変更する、異なる
- **Vega** 名 ベガ、織女星
- **vegetable** 名 野菜、青物 形 野菜の、植物(性)の
- **Vernal Equinox** 名 春分
- **vertical** 形 垂直の、縦の 名 垂直線
- **victim** 名 犠牲者、被害者
- **vinegar** 名 ビネガー、酢
- **visitor** 名 訪問客
- **vocabulary** 名 ①語彙 ②単語集
- **volcano** 名 火山、噴火口
- **volt** 名 ボルト《電圧の単位》
- **volunteer** 名 志願者、ボランティア 動 自発的に申し出る
- **vote** 名 投票(権)、票決 動 投票する、~を投票して決める
- **voter** 名 投票者
- **vow** 名 誓い、誓約 動 誓う

W

- **ward** 名 行政区
- **warlord** 名 軍事的指導者、(日本の)戦国大名
- **warn** 動 警告する、用心させる
- **warring-state** 名 戦争状態
- **warrior** 名 戦士、軍人
- **Washington** 名 ワシントン《地名》
- **watchdog** 名 番犬、監視人
- **waterfall** 名 滝、ドッと押し寄せるもの
- **wax** 名 ろう、ワックス 動 ワックスで磨く
- **wealthy** 形 裕福な、金持ちの
- **weapon** 名 武器、兵器 動 ~を武装させる、~に武器を供給する
- **wedding** 名 結婚式、婚礼
- **weigh** 動 ①(重さ)をはかる、比較検討する ②圧迫する、重荷である
- **well-organized** 形 うまく(きちんと)組織化されて
- **western** 形 ①西の、西側の ②西洋の
- **western-style** 形 西洋風の
- **whatever** 代 ①~するものは何でも ②どんなこと[もの]が~とも 形 ①どんな~でも ②《否定文、疑問文で》少しの~も、何らかの
- **wheat** 名 小麦
- **whenever** 接 ①~するときはいつでも、~するたびに ②いつ~しても 副 一体いつ
- **whether** 接 ~かどうか、~かまたは…、~であろうとなかろうと
- **whole** 形 全体の、すべての、完全な、満~、丸~ 名 《the –》全体、全部
- **wholesale** 名 卸売り 形 卸の、大規模な
- **wide** 形 幅の広い、広範囲の 副 広く、大きく開いて

Word List

- **wildlife** 名野生生物
- **willing** 形《be – to ~》快く~する,~するのをいとわない
- **wine** 名ワイン,ぶどう酒
- **within** 前①~の中[内]に,~の内部に ②~以内で,~を越えないで 副中[内]へ[に],内部に 名内部
- **woke** 動 wake（目がさめる）の過去
- **work out** 熟何とかなる,うまくいく
- **worker** 名働く人,労働者
- **worker-household** 名勤労者世帯
- **working-class** 形労働者階級の
- **workplace** 名職場,仕事場
- **World Heritage Sites** 名世界遺産登録地
- **world-famous** 形世界的に有名な
- **worse** 形いっそう悪い,より劣った,よりひどい 副いっそう悪く
- **worst** 形《the –》最も悪い,一番ひどい 副最も悪く,一番ひどく 名《the –》最悪の事態[人,物]
- **wrestle** 動取っ組み合う,格闘する
- **wrestler** 名レスラー
- **wrestling** 名レスリング,格闘

E-CAT

English **C**onversational **A**bility **T**est
国際英語会話能力検定

● E-CATとは…
英語が話せるようになるためのテストです。インターネットベースで、30分であなたの発話力をチェックします。

www.ecatexam.com

iTEP

● iTEP®とは…
世界各国の企業、政府機関、アメリカの大学300校以上が、英語能力判定テストとして採用。オンラインによる90分のテストで文法、リーディング、リスニング、ライティング、スピーキングの5技能をスコア化。iTEP®は、留学、就職、海外赴任などに必要な、世界に通用する英語力を総合的に評価する画期的なテストです。

www.itepexamjapan.com

ラダーシリーズ
Japan FAQ（Frequently Asked Questions）ジャパン FAQ

2005年 9月10日　第 1 刷発行
2023年 4月 1 日　第15刷発行

著　者　ディビッド・セイン

発行者　浦　　晋亮

発行所　IBCパブリッシング株式会社
　　　　〒162-0804 東京都新宿区中里町 29 番 3 号
　　　　菱秀神楽坂ビル
　　　　Tel. 03-3513-4511　Fax. 03-3513-4512
　　　　www.ibcpub.co.jp

© David Thayne 2005
© IBC Publishing, Inc. 2005

印刷　株式会社シナノパブリッシングプレス
装丁　伊藤 理恵
編集協力　足立 恵子（サイクルズ・カンパニー）
組版データ　Minion Pro Regular + Frutiger 65 Bold

落丁本・乱丁本は、小社宛にお送りください。送料小社負担にてお取り替えいたします。本書の無断複写（コピー）は著作権法上での例外を除き禁じられています。

Printed in Japan
ISBN978-4-89684-034-6